"Here are the lessons you want your children to learn and the tools and foundation for personal fulfillment."
—Luka Erceg, Founder of Simbol Materials

"As a former US Army Special Forces operator (the Green Berets), an entrepreneur, and a father, I highly recommend this book. Mills does a masterful job of embedding the mission-critical components of how to succeed at anything in a wonderful storyline that is both memorable and remarkable. Put this book on your required reading list!"
—Larry Broughton, Founder and CEO,
broughtonHOTELS.com and BROUGHTONadvisory.com

"Reading BE UNSTOPPABLE is like getting a Royal flush every time you play poker, except it's better. Mills removes the mystery from success with a wonderfully simple code that you can apply to anything you have the courage to go after. This is a book that you will read over and over!"
—Annie Duke, Professional Poker Player,
World Series of Poker Gold Bracelet Winner

"This book teaches what most people in their heart of hearts know to be true. However, knowing achieves nothing. Only action leads to success and that's where this book scores so high. Through clever fable it guides and motivates to action."
—Mike Faith, CEO, Headsets.com, Inc.

"Alden infused this important work with energy, practical thinking, and a challenge for anyone looking for real change. I look forward to applying these principles to my own business and life."
—David R. Duncan, President and CEO,
Silver Oak and Twomey Cellars

"I plan to read this to my daughter at least a few times. I recommend this book to parents, and to anyone who wants to get more out of their life."
—Chris Caren, father of one, CEO of Turnitin.com, the leading academic plagiarism checker technology for teachers and students

"The bad news is that this book wasn't available when I was playing football! The good news is that it will be mandatory reading for all three of my children."
—Damon Huard, NFL quarterback, two-time
NFL Super Bowl champion

BE
UNSTOPPABLE

BE
UNSTOPPABLE

The 8 Essential
Actions to
Succeed at Anything

by

Alden Mills

Tilbury House Publishers
Thomaston, Maine

Be Unstoppable: The Eight Essential Actions to Succeed at Anything

Tilbury House Publishers
12 Starr St.
Thomaston, ME 04861
800-582-1899 • www.tilburyhouse.com

Copyright © 2013 and 2017 by Alden M. Mills

Library of Congress Control Number: 2017930358

ISBN 978-0-88448-530-8 (hc)
ISBN 978-0-88448-535-3 (eBook)

Cover design by Thomas Rainwater
Interior design and illustrations by Dan Kirchoff
Author photo by Kevin Erdman

Printed in the United States of America

17 18   MAP   10 9 8 7 6 5

Contents

For our Captains-in-Training,
H-master, Chow-chow, Bear, and Yum-yum
Never, ever give up on your dreams!
Love, Mom and Dad

"Go confidently in the direction of your dreams!
Live the life you've imagined."
— Henry David Thoreau

"The future belongs to those
who believe in the beauty of their dreams."
— Eleanor Roosevelt

Introduction

My inspiration and purpose for writing this book comes from my boys — all four of them. As their mother and I proudly watch them grow, and test our patience by purposely not listening to our spoken words, I'm hopeful the written word might have a more lasting impact. Like most parents, we want our children to succeed. We want to give them the tools for success, including a good education and a full array of life skills from swimming to not hitting their brothers to flossing their teeth. As we navigate parenthood without a map or playbook, life doesn't wait for us to adapt; it just happens.

A lot has happened since I made the decision to leave the SEAL teams and start my own business. For starters, several of my SEAL teammates are no longer with us. Back then we prepared "just-in-case" letters to be sent to our loved ones if we didn't return from a mission. In mine, I would thank my parents for the gifts they had given me, which enabled me to do what I loved doing most at that moment: leading SEALs. I would tell them not to be upset—that if the letter had been sent, it meant that I had died doing what I loved, and how many people are privileged to say that? I always wrote a letter to my younger brother, Andrew, usually starting it with a laundry list of apologies. Sorry for throwing a rock at your head in third grade, sorry for pretending to drown you at the lake, sorry for breaking your favorite Matchbox cars, and (the one I will always regret most) sorry for missing your wedding. But I always tried to end on a positive note, telling him how proud of him I was for his overcoming dyslexia, and that he could do anything he put his mind to. I would tell him to keep trying and never to give up, and to know that even though I was no longer physically there for him, I would always be with him in spirit, cheering him on.

Thankfully, none of those letters ever needed to be sent from my platoons, but that hasn't been the case for many SEAL teammates. And many of those letters weren't addressed to mothers, fathers, brothers, sisters, girlfriends, or wives; they were addressed to sons and daughters. Though I no longer serve in harm's way, I think daily about my fallen teammates and wonder what they wrote to their children and what wisdom they would have shared if given the chance. It was this thinking that inspired this book. It's my "just-in-case" letter to my boys.

I was doing what I loved back in those SEAL days, and I had the confidence of knowing I could do anything I put my mind to. I want this book to capture those themes in a way my boys and everyone else who reads it will remember. A collection of vignettes could illustrate how anyone can accomplish great things, but would it leave a lasting impression? I've tried to create a framework, a code my sons can follow throughout their lives, a touchstone to encourage them when the going gets tough. I want this book to capture the essence of my spirit as a tangible reference for them, a pick-me-up when they feel like giving up on a dream, a voice of encouragement when no one else believes in them, or perhaps simply the voice of a proud father saying, "Go for it — you can do it!"

I've spent the better part of the last four years thinking about what this book should be. In the end I settled on three ideas to make it memorable and, hopefully, to inspire others to go after their dreams. The first idea was to decipher and distill the essence of how I was able to beat asthma, become a rowing champion, lead Navy SEALs, and create the fastest-growing consumer products company in the United States (in 2009). What I realized by analyzing these pivotal successes in my life was that in each of them I unknowingly put eight actions into motion. Over time (and lots of it), I refined those actions into a simple, easy-to-remember code called U.P.E.R.S.I.S.T., as explained in the eight chapters of this book.

The second challenge was determining how to teach the code in a memorable way without losing the reader (my boys and you) in the process. I decided that a parable would offer the most memorable and engaging way to introduce the code, and what better way to build a connection with the reader and the code than to use the metaphor of a captain and his ship?

The final component of this book was developed to provide readers with the ability to implement each of the eight actions immediately. There's no time like the present to start making your dreams happen, and this book should encourage you to take action ASAP! This is the reasoning behind the "How to Get Started" section at the end of each chapter. I include short insights into my SEAL and entrepreneurial experiences in each of these eight sections to help demonstrate how these actions can work for anyone going after their dreams.

Speaking of dreams, if you remember nothing else from this book, remember this: *"YOUR LIFE IS UP TO YOU. YOU DECIDE WHAT KIND OF LIFE YOU LIVE!"*

Those words, I now realize, have guided me throughout my life. I decided not to listen to the doctor who said that, due to my asthma, I should learn to play chess instead of playing outside. I decided to work harder so I could pull harder than other rowers and earn the opportunity to win a gold medal at the New England Championships and the Olympic Festival. I decided not to quit when more than 80 percent of my classmates rang out of SEAL training. I decided to invent the Perfect Pushup when my investors told me to get a job. In each of my most important successes in life, the key was not giving up on a dream. And the key to not giving up on a dream is understanding why you want to make that dream come true. The better you understand your "why," the better able you will be to persist when others give up on you. When you come to understand your "why," you *will* figure out your way. And once you do this, you will come to appreciate that we have only two limitations in life: our imagination and determination.

Dreaming isn't difficult (especially when you're young). It's the follow-up that's hard, and that's where I know this book will come in handy. The sad truth is that few dreams ever become reality. Why is that? Simply put, the answer is in your head. Your mind can be your best friend or your worst enemy, and it's the deciding factor on what kind of life you live. Your mind isn't pre-programmed to tell you what to do with the dreams it conjures up. Your mind is only as good as the inputs it receives. If the chief input is a constant stream of "you can't," then your dream is dead on arrival. But if the inputs streaming in begin with "you can," your dreams have a chance of becoming real. And the most important inputs, the ones that matter most, are the ones your mind gives itself.

Unfortunately, essential though it is, the power of positive input isn't all you need to succeed. Your master and commander, your mind, needs more input to be convinced to work at making a dream real. That's why I wrote this book. It will give your mind a code to follow so that no matter what obstacle attempts to derail you, your mind will be working for you, not against you. And when your mind is on your side, no obstacle is too big, no dream too daunting, and nothing can stop you from living an amazing life!

Once you've mastered the code in this book, your biggest challenge will be dreaming bigger dreams! That's right: Once you've tasted success and gained the confidence of making a dream come true, a funny thing happens: You get addicted to making dreams come true. And as each dream gets a little bigger and a little scarier, you get stronger, smarter, and better at making them come true. And isn't that what life is all about? Live your dreams!

Dream on boys, *you can do it!*

I love you, Dad.

The town of Uptoyou is unique. Every resident owns a boat. From oldest to youngest, in the town of Uptoyou every person gets a boat the day he or she is born, and the good citizens of Uptoyou keep their boats until the day they die. Their lives are spent learning how to captain their boats. These boats are unlike any boat you can buy, each one is slightly different; they are unique to the individual, but all function the same way. Another interesting feature is Uptoyou boats grow with you and you can change your boat as you grow. Uptoyou boats can be made faster, bigger to carry more things, or tougher to handle bigger seas. Uptoyou boats can be changed to do whatever you want your boat to do, but making changes to your boat takes time and commitment, and the bigger the change, the longer the wait.

All children born in the town of Uptoyou go to Uptoyou Univer-

Prologue to a
Sea Story

sity, where they learn how to be captains of their boats. They are taught the basics of seamanship and navigation; how to navigate, drive, maintain, and improve their boats, and how to make money with them. By the time students graduate from Uptoyou University, they are ready to test their new skills in the busiest port in the world, Hardwork Harbor. Hardwork Harbor is where all the people of Uptoyou go to work and play. From ferry boats and cargo boats to boats exploring the world, Hardwork Harbor has a place for everyone's boat.

Recently, two boys named Tim and Ted graduated from Uptoyou University. Tim and Ted had grown up on the same street in the town of Uptoyou and had been friends for as long as they could remember. They both had dreams of high adventure, captaining their boats around the globe in search of fun, fortune, and fame. But though they grew up on the same street, went to the same school, and received the same degree, Tim and Ted weren't the same. Nothing came easy for Tim. He had to work harder than Ted at everything. At times, Tim felt that life wasn't fair because he had to work so much harder than Ted at just about everything he did, whether getting good grades in school or boating on the water.

There were other differences between Tim and Ted. Ted loved to talk about everything he did. He boasted about how easy everything was for him. He bragged about what he would do after leaving university, about how he would travel the world in his boat, invent things that everyone would need for their boats, and become rich and famous. No one doubted Ted; he made everything look easy, and it made sense that he would succeed in Hardwork Harbor. Ted was popular and had lots of friends.

Tim wasn't nearly as popular as Ted, but Tim claimed Ted a friend because they had grown up next door to each other. Tim had dreams too, but he kept them to himself. He didn't want people to laugh at his dreams of sailing the seven seas. And laugh they would if they had known what he really wanted to do, since he had barely passed the university navigation exams. When graduation finally arrived, Ted won the award for most likely to succeed in Hardwork Harbor. Everybody thought Ted was terrific. Tim didn't win any awards, but he did get exactly the same degree as Ted, and both of them graduated with exactly the same education. Both of them were captains.

When Tim and Ted launched their boats at Hardwork Harbor, both were very excited about their future as captains. Of course, Ted told everyone what he planned to do as captain of his boat, while Tim kept his plans to himself. Their first weeks of work were new and exciting for both of them. They had the same job ferrying cargo from one side of the harbor to the other. Tim found the work challenging but rewarding. He had to work hard to keep up with the fleet of other boats while learning how to navigate the waters of Hardwork Harbor. The waters were different from what he had studied in school. Every week the waters seemed to present new challenges for the young captains. Sandbars were never in the same place for very long. To make matters even more difficult, the winds and waves were constantly shifting, making the two captains work harder to get back and forth with their loads.

Tim loved the challenge. No two days were the same. Ted, on the other hand, started to get frustrated. As soon as he thought he had figured out the best route to the other side of the harbor, he had to relearn it the next week. Ted also was getting frustrated with his first job. He was destined for greatness; everybody at school had told him so, so why should someone like him have to do this lowly cargo job when he should be navigating the high seas with precious cargo headed to foreign harbors?

After a few weeks of work, the young captains met with older captains of the cargo company. The older captains offered them all kinds of advice, from how to better carry their cargoes to how to read the waters so they could avoid running aground. Tim listened to the crusty, seasoned captains. He took notes and asked lots of questions. He respected the older captains' experience and realized that they could help him become better at his job. Tim was looking for all the help he could get, but Ted didn't think he needed any help. After all, some of these captains hadn't even graduated from Uptoyou University, let alone won awards as Ted had done. What could these captains know that he did not?

As the weeks turned into months, something interesting started to happen. At first it was barely noticeable, but every once in a while Tim would finish his day of cargo carrying before Ted. Even though they carried exactly the same loads over exactly the same routes. Prior to this, Tim had never beaten Ted at anything. Ted had always been first at everything he did, and he liked to remind Tim of that. But now things were slowly changing. On the days Tim beat Ted, Tim would never mention it to anyone, but Ted would go out of his way to offer up reasons why Tim had completed his work first. Ted would only talk to Tim when other captains were within earshot, saying that he had run his boat slower to save fuel or had stopped to chat with some other captain. Ted had never complimented Tim on anything Tim had accomplished at school, and it was no different on the waters of Hardwork Harbor.

After a year, however, Tim was consistently finishing his work before Ted. The older captains noticed this and offered Tim more responsibility: a new course with more cargo. The day this news got around was the day Ted stopped liking Tim. Ted told anyone who would listen that the senior cargo captains didn't like him, that the older captains were jealous of Ted's natural abilities, and that's why he didn't get the bigger cargoes and the longer routes. He even told his former friend that the only reason Tim got the job over Ted was that the senior captains felt sorry for Tim. While Ted was busy making excuses to anyone who would listen, Tim was busy making changes to his boat to handle the increased workload. Tim needed to make his boat a little bigger and a little stronger to handle the bigger cargo and the longer course. Tim struggled with learning how to navigate his ship with the new workload, often working on weekends practicing his docking skills or learning new navigational methods to carry him through the deeper waters. He needed to change his boat to adapt to the new challenges. The change was exciting but frustrating, frightening, and a lot of work.

Tim had just become comfortable with his expanded cargo course when the older captains offered him a chance to navigate a course across the bay of Hardwork Harbor to the North. The new course made Tim nervous. It had taken him the better part of a year to master the east/west route across Hardwork Harbor. The new course called for new northerly headings. Only a small portion of his old course would be included in his new route across the bay, and the new headings would require him to take seas broadside while crossing the bay, a first for Tim. He tossed and turned in his sleep in the nights before embarking on the new course as all kinds of questions bounced about in his head. How long would it take to master this course? Would he even be able to make it there? What if he ran his boat aground? What if his boat sank? These questions never seemed to stop; he couldn't stop focusing on all the things that could go wrong. By the time Tim was ready to depart on his new course, he was a nervous wreck.

The day Tim ran his new course was the single worst day he'd ever had on the water. Ted and his fleet of friends showed up to wish Tim luck, but with smirks on their faces. Tim knew they weren't there to be supportive; they were there to watch him fail. Tim was so nervous when he motored away from the pier that he forgot to untie one of his dock lines, and the results were a parted line, a bent cleat, and a harbor full of laughter from Ted and his friends.

Once away from Ted and the others, Tim was able to relax; the first leg of the new course was the same course he had navigated all through the previous year. He knew these waters. But it wasn't long before he had to turn his boat onto a new heading into seas he didn't know. At first, the course change didn't seem like a big deal, but then the winds changed and the seas built, causing waves to start breaking over his port side. The entire boat shuddered and wallowed as it plowed into one large wave after another. Tim started to panic; he'd never been in seas like this, and he was scared that his boat wouldn't be able to handle the conditions. He started to repeat aloud the questions from his sleepless nights. While he was panicking on the bridge, he wasn't paying attention to his navigation, and by the time he realized that he'd slipped out of the channel, it was too late to avoid what came next. Tim saw the sandbar lining the starboard boundary of the channel at the same moment that he heard the grinding of his bow as it dug into the hard sand. Tim tried to back his boat off the bar, but between the broadside seas and his heavy cargo, his engines were too weak to break the boat free.

Tim sat trembling in shock on the bridge for a good couple of minutes, trying to avoid what he knew he had to do: make a distress call for help. He was less worried about getting off the sandbar than about having the entire harbor hear his call for help. He was sure this call would cost him any chance he had with the cargo company, and he could only imagine how much teasing he would have to endure from Ted and his fleet of "Wanna-be-like-Ted" friends. Tim was sick to his stomach as he made the distress call. "This is Captain Tim requesting...ah...assistance, over." His voice was feeble and uncertain as it was broadcast over the radio channel that all of the harbor captains monitored.

Within seconds of Tim's call, he recognized the voice of the responder. "Captain Tim, this is Captain Bill. Please advise what kind of assistance is required, over." It was the very cargo captain who had offered Tim the new course. Tim was crushed. He needed a solid minute to gather his muffled response: "A...a...a...tow."

Captain Bill didn't hesitate; he requested Tim's exact location and confirmed that he was on his way to assist. But it took a good two hours for Captain Bill to arrive, and while Tim waited, he continued in vain to rev his engines in an attempt to free his ship from the bar. By the time the older captain arrived, Tim's attempts to free himself had caused additional damage to his propellers. No longer did he just need a tow off the bar; now he needed a tow to his destination.

Captain Bill kept his radio transmissions to a minimum as he and Tim coordinated the tow, but their communications were sufficient to alert Ted and his buddies on shore to what had happened.

To make matters worse, while Tim was under tow, he had to keep his shipboard radio on to ensure that he and Captain Bill could communicate, which also meant that he had to endure Ted and his buddies' relentless quips about the incident. Tim felt that this was the single worst day of his life. He was mortified. He didn't ever want to leave his boat, and he wondered how long he could live onboard so as not to have to face another captain again. Maybe he could just drop anchor in the middle of the bay as some of the other captains had done, and only row ashore at night to get provisions so he could avoid as many captains as possible. Tim continued to chart out his plan for hiding from as many people as possible as the older captain towed him to a berth in his destination harbor. He was so upset he couldn't even look Captain Bill in the eye to say thank you as he hurriedly untied the towline from the bow of his boat. The older captain didn't say a word once he was certain Tim was safely tied to the pier. He tilted his cap at Tim and headed back on the southerly route to Hardwork Harbor.

As Tim hid on the bridge and watched his cargo being unloaded while the sun poured late-afternoon rays of light across the bay, a ship silently eased into the slip beside his. At first Tim didn't want to look at the ship for fear he might make eye contact with the captain and be subjected to more jokes and ridicule for his grounding in the middle of the bay. But that thought left him quickly. The hardware and brightwork of the visiting vessel glistened as if someone were using a signaling mirror to capture his attention. The reflection was so startling and bright that Tim had to put his hand up to cover his eyes.

As his eyes adapted to the shimmering reflections, his jaw dropped, and he slowly rose to his feet to get a better view of the magnificent ship pulling in just ahead of his bow. Momentarily forgetting his depression, Tim stared in amazement at the most incredible ship he had ever seen. The shine from the stainless steel railings, cleats, horns, bells, anchors, capstans, and portholes was the source of the sun's brilliant reflections. But there was so much more to take in, starting with the high flared bow coated in onyx black marine paint, with a blood-red boottop stripe marking where the black hull met the water. Tim's eyes danced from stem to stern, trying to capture and comprehend all the features of this remarkable vessel. There were massive satellite domes above the bridge; dual sets of matching anchors on the bow and stern; oiled teak decks and varnished teak handrails and trim; and graceful hull and cabin lines that flowed like a rolling wave from stem to stern. She was a masterpiece. Tim stood in complete silence, his mouth agape and eyes wide as the captain masterfully commanded his ship into the slip. Tim couldn't believe his eyes; he had no idea a boat like this could even exist, let alone be moored one slip away from his own!

Tim was in a daze on his bridge as he read the large, brass-colored letters that arced across the teak transom of this one-of-a-kind ship: *Persistence*. Tim was so lost in daydreaming about the capabilities of this grand ship that he almost didn't hear the ship's captain call over to him in a hearty voice, "Ahoy there, Captain!"

What Tim saw

Tim looked awkwardly behind himself and thought, *Who is this captain calling to? He couldn't be speaking to me, could he?* Finally he replied with a crackle in his voice, "Ahh, ahoy, sir."

The captain of the *Persistence* was much older than Tim but spoke with a youthful energy. "Say there, Captain, I've been at sea for many months and haven't been back to Hardwork Harbor for years. Are you from around here?"

Tim was so startled by the other captain's eagerness to chat with him that he fumbled his response, saying, "No. I ... I mean ... yes." Tim felt his cheeks flush with embarrassment and tried to clarify by stating, "I'm from Hardwork Harbor, on the southern side of the bay, and this is my first visit to the northern side."

"Well, welcome to Hardwork Harbor North!" the other captain said with a smile, and continued, "Say, do you like fried clams and chowder?"

Tim cocked his head back and to the right as if to say, "Who doesn't like fried clams and chowder?," but his actual response was only a slow nod of the head and a meager "Sure."

"Great! There's a clam shack at the end of the pier that had the best fried clams and chowder this side of the harbor, and I'm happy to report it's still there. How about joining me for some? I'd love to hear what's been happening in Hardwork Harbor!" The senior captain smiled encouragingly as he waited for a response.

Tim muttered quietly to himself, "Where have you been all those years? I have never met someone who has left Hardwork Harbor for years at a time." As Tim was processing the captain's last transmission, a question popped into his head: *Why would a captain of such a grand ship want to spend any time with a captain of a small ship such as mine? Surely he won't want to spend any time with me once he finds out I was the one who ran aground today.* And as Tim was nodding to himself, he heard the captain exclaim, "Terrific! I'll meet you on the pier in five minutes." Tim was terrified. He had accidentally said yes! He had never been to dinner with such a clearly important person. His mind raced with questions. What could he possibly talk to this worldly captain about? What would the captain think of him after finding out that it had been Tim who had run aground that day? He thought about declining the invitation and was about to make up some excuse about needing to work on his boat when he heard the captain walking onto the gangway of his very own boat!

"Hi ya, Captain, name's Peter. Mind if I come aboard for a minute? I used to have a boat just like this one!" Tim was shell-shocked as he extended his hand and received a firm, energetic handshake from Peter. "Hi, sir. I'm, ah...Tim. Welcome aboard, sir." Tim felt meek in the presence of this impressive captain. Peter responded without hesitation, "What's all this 'sir' business? We're both captains! Please call me Peter." And with that, Peter asked Tim for a tour of his boat and peppered Tim with questions about everything from the harbor to the changes Tim was making to his boat. Peter seemed interested in everything Tim had to say. He even complimented Tim on his boat! Tim couldn't believe it. This made Tim relax and gave him the confidence to ask Peter, "Could I tour your boat?"

"Why of course, Tim! I'd be delighted to give you a tour of the *Persistence*." Peter saw the immediate impact the invitation had on

Tim. It was as if Tim became a different person. He came alive with excitement, and his enthusiasm was contagious. Peter smiled broadly back at the young captain as they stepped aboard the *Persistence*. Tim couldn't believe his eyes. This was the grandest boat he'd ever set foot on. Everything about the boat was incredible. She had perfect in-laid teak decks and massive anchors attached to automated stainless steel winches, and her decks were protected by the highest flared bow he'd ever seen. As Tim toured the bow, he noticed large steel plates welded to the outside of the hull. He imagined how easily this boat would have handled the waves he'd dealt with earlier that day.

As the tour continued, Tim noticed other unusual modifications, such as a massive engine connected to an equally massive anchor on the stern of the boat. In the engine room there were two diesel engines connected to rows of batteries, and on the bridge there were more electronic systems than he had ever known existed. Peter showed him a radar system that could look over the horizon at ships heading his way, a sonar system that could detect submerged obstacles hundreds of meters in front of the boat, and a night-vision system that allowed a captain to see in the darkest of nights for a mile in any direction. Tim couldn't help but daydream about this ship's awesome capabilities. The more he learned about the *Persistence*, the more he wanted to know how he could turn his boat into a ship like this one. Captain Peter had spent a lifetime improving his boat, and it showed. The *Persistence* was prepared for anything.

As they toured the wardroom and galley, Tim couldn't help but stare at all the exotic artifacts adorning the walls. There were handmade spears, animal figurines carved from bone and stone, colorful paintings of majestic lands with snow-white sand beaches and turquoise waters teeming with brilliantly colored fish, hand-woven baskets and beautiful wooden bowls, and a remarkable life-like painting of a captain and his ship heading into a ferocious storm. Peter's wardroom was more like a gallery of fine art than a dining room; Tim was overwhelmed with curiosity.

Finally Peter saw Tim's astonishment at the things he was seeing and broke the silence. "You know, Tim, I grew up in the town of Uptoyou, too. Had a boat just like yours at your age, and even did that same job you're doing now."

"You did, really?" Tim said with a dumbfounded look on this face. "But how is this possible? I've never seen another boat like yours in Hardwork Harbor before."

"Tim, have you ever left Hardwork Harbor before?"

"Well, I've thought of leaving the harbor, but I haven't yet," said Tim sheepishly.

"Totally understandable. I didn't leave Hardwork Harbor until I was older than you. It took me a good long while to get up enough courage to leave the harbor. I'll never forget everyone telling me how crazy I was. They said I was sure to die with my boat shipwrecked in some faraway place or, worse yet, swallowed by a sea monster. It seems pretty funny to me now, looking back on it, but at the time it scared me."

Tim knew exactly what Peter was talking about. Although Tim hadn't told any of his friends that he had dreams of leaving the harbor someday, he could only imagine how much fun they would make of him, especially considering how they'd treated him after running aground. Tim nodded his head slowly at Peter's confession and asked, "So why did you leave the Harbor?"

Peter turned to Tim as they headed back to the pier, grinned, and said, "Well, there was this one night when I was working late on my boat, making repairs actually, because I had run aground earlier that day, when . . . "

"Wait a second, you ran aground, too?" Tim nearly shouted in astonishment to Peter.

Peter laughed heartily and replied with a chuckle, "If you gave me a dollar for every time I've run aground, I'd be the richest man in Hardwork Harbor! I ran aground so many times that my so-called friends gave me a helmet so I wouldn't hurt myself on the bridge. My attitude is, if you don't run aground from time to time, then you're not trying hard enough!"

Tim stood with his mouth open and his eyes nearly popping out of their sockets as Peter's words registered with him. Peter laughed and said, "C'mon sailor, let's go get some chowder and fried clams, and I'll tell you all about it. I'm starving!"

Peter was halfway down the gangway before Tim started following him. Peter's pace surprised Tim; for an older captain he certainly walked with a spring in his step. They continued in relative silence as both of them took in the sights the waterfront walk offered them on their way to Jack's Clam Shack. As they walked inside the dilapidated shack covered with lobster pot buoys, Peter closed his eyes for a moment, took an exaggerated sniff through his nostrils, and smiled at the familiar smells of the shack. "Smells just the way I remember it!" Peter flashed a smile as he turned to his young companion and stated, "A cup of clam chowder and the fried-clam platter is the only way to go, skipper." Tim, who was still taking the restaurant in and attempting to find a menu, responded with, "Ah, sounds good to me. Count me in for the same."

While Captain Peter ordered, Tim finally found the menu; it was scratched in white chalk on a green board that rested on top of two lobster pots. It read:

Chowdah — made fresh daily
Full-belly Clams only
Lobstah when we have it — we don't have it
All meals come with fries and slaw — no substitutions
Cash Only: If you have to ask how much, then this isn't the place for you.
Jack

Tim was taken aback by how short and curt the menu was, and was just about to say as much when Peter, seeming to read his thoughts, said, "Isn't it a great menu? Simple and to the point. Good ole Captain Jack knew exactly what he wanted when he built this restaurant, and I love this place — authentic to the core."

Tim nodded slowly and said quietly under his breath, "Yep, it's definitely one of a kind." Just then he heard a voice bellow, "Shiver me clam shells, look what the tide brought in: P-Squared!"

A mountain of a man leaned over the counter to embrace Captain Peter. The man wore an old white apron that was more brown than white from years of fryer and clam batter stains. His hands and forearms were covered in flour. Tim could make out faded tattoos on both of his forearms as he grabbed Peter in a massive bear hug.

Jack's Clam Shack

"So good to see you, Jack!" Peter exclaimed as he returned the bear hug.

"How many moons has it been, P2? Twelve to eighteen, at least!" Jack said as he grabbed Peter by his shoulders to get a good look at him.

"I'd say about sixteen moons by your count, Jack. Couldn't make it to eighteen. Started going into *chowdah* and fried clam withdrawals!" Peter said with a wink and a smile. Turning toward Tim, he said, "Jack, I'd like you to meet a first-timer to your fine establishment. Meet Tim."

"Ahoy there, Tim, good to meet ya. Hope you brought your appetite, 'cause you're in for a treat tonight!" Jack said as his hand engulfed Tim's and squeezed it so hard it made Tim wince. As Jack motioned Peter and Tim to a table directly in front of an old mahogany ship's wheel mated with a brass compass — clearly the table of distinction — he asked with a toothy grin, "So Double-P, what brings ya' in? Surely you've reverse-engineered my secret clam batter recipe by now."

Peter responded with a warm tap on Jack's shoulder. "Jack, old Double-P here gave up trying to figure out your recipe long ago. You have nothing to fear. That's one recipe Pierre-deuce will never master. As for what brings me 'in,' I need to do a little tweak to the *Persistence*. I hear the boys down the pier might be able to make her just a little less thirsty."

Jack nodded his head slowly and laughed softly as he said, "You never change, do you, ole boy. Still making improvements, aren't ya'?" As Peter nodded slightly, Jack turned to Tim and said, "Son, soak up every last word this captain offers you. My chowdah and clams may be the best, but there's no skipper on the planet finer than the one you're sitting next to right now."

Jack's jovial tone had turned serious as he spoke to the young captain. Tim was startled by this sudden change in intensity, and sat a little straighter in his chair as he said, "Aye, aye, Jack."

"Thatta boy. Keep that attitude and you just might learn something that will change your life." Jack raised his eyebrows and tilted his head as he leaned forward to offer this bit of advice; it was as if he were sharing a secret with the young man. Satisfied that his message had been received, Jack turned his attention back to Peter.

"Well, my friend, all's good here. Still living the dream, as I'm sure you are. I'd love to stay and chat, but I got clams to fry! So I'll leave you to it, but promise me you'll stop by before lunch tomorrow so you can get me caught up on your latest courses. Promise me P-P!" demanded Jack. Jack didn't move until he heard Peter commit to meet him the next day. Peter smiled and said, "Have I ever left without saying goodbye, my old friend?"

"Point taken. Can't wait to catch up! Now, make sure the youngster here doesn't fill up on oyster crackers before the best meal of his life arrives!" commanded the proud chef. As Jack walked away, a series of questions whirled through the young skipper's brain. What was with all the nicknames for Peter — P-Squared, P2, Double-P, P-P, Pierre-deuce? And how did Jack think that listening to Peter could change his life? Before he could ask Peter these things, the older skipper looked at him and said, "I love his energy, always upbeat. And I promise, you'll love his food."

Tim nodded and responded with, "He's definitely fired up about his fried clams. Never met anyone more motivated about chowder and clams."

"That's what makes this restaurant special, Tim. I'm not kidding you when I say that captains from around the globe make detours from their courses to enjoy a meal at Jack's Shack. And do you know why?"

"He uses a special batter recipe and fresh clams?" guessed Tim.

"It certainly helps to have great ingredients, but that's not the real reason his restaurant makes captains change their courses. The real reason is that he loves what he does. You can't fake his kind of passion — it's infectious. People want to be around someone like him. He finds joy in serving the very best chowder and fried clams. That's his course, and people want to be along for the ride with him," explained Peter.

Tim leaned forward nervously on the old wooden table and slowly nodded, trying to focus on what his table mate had just said. Peter could see from Tim's body language that his words weren't quite registering, so he tried a different tack. "Okay, let's get back to the topic we started exploring before my stomach interrupted us: running aground."

Tim shot bolt upright in his chair at the words "running aground" and said, "Have you really run aground more than once?"

Peter couldn't help himself as he leaned back and laughed out loud in his chair. "Yes, I've run aground more than once." The salty skipper leaned forward, placed his hand on Tim's shoulder, and continued. "You see, the way I see it, the important thing about running aground is making sure you understand *why* you ran aground. When you understand the 'why,' then you'll figure out the 'way' not to do it again — at least on that particular leg of your course."

"I'm not sure I'm tracking with you, Peter. What do you mean about the 'why' and the 'way'?"

"Understanding the 'why' is the single most important thing you, as captain of your ship, can do. This goes far beyond running aground. Understanding the 'why' in anything you do will give you the purpose to accomplish anything you want; understanding the 'why' is what will keep you going when everyone else gives up. Once you understand the 'why,' then you can work on figuring out the 'way' to get something done," Peter stated matter-of-factly. "Look, Tim, I ran aground so many times because I was trying new courses, or I was trying to do something a little better, a little faster than the other captains. My boat wasn't as fast or as strong as other boats in the harbor, so the only way I could keep up with the bigger boats was to find new, shorter routes. Sometimes it worked, a lot of times it didn't. But here's the key: Why was I trying so hard in the first place? Many of my friends thought I was foolish. They didn't understand why I was willing to take these risks."

Tim interrupted. "So why *were* you willing to take those risks?"

Peter smiled and said, "Well, taking those risks goes back to what happened to me after I ran my boat aground the first time. I met a captain. Well, actually he was more than a captain, but I didn't realize it at the time."

"Huh?" said Tim. "I didn't realize there was *anything* above a captain."

"There sure is, Tim, and it's called a 'master and commander.' Technically speaking, we're all captains, but a master and commander takes orders from no one. A master and commander has become so good at being a captain that he or she runs his own ship without the support of a larger fleet. Masters and commanders have become so proficient at running their boats that they can find work wherever they cruise."

"Whoa," said Tim. "I had no idea you could do that. Are there many of these masters and commanders around?"

"Yes there are, but don't be alarmed that you haven't met any. They don't cruise in a fleet or, for that matter, with other captains. They're all following their own courses," stated Captain Peter. "And many of them make a habit of stopping at Jack's," he said with a wink and a smile. "Now, about why I was taking those risks to find faster ways around the harbor. As I was saying, I was sulking around the harbor, having just run aground for the first time, when I laid eyes on a ship the likes of which I had never seen before. It coasted into the berth right next to mine, and much like you and I met, the captain, a friendly older fellow, saw my keen interest in his ship and invited me aboard. I asked him all kinds of questions but mostly marveled at his ship and the places he had taken her — all around the world it seemed, and to places I had never heard of. I knew that night that I wanted to live a life like that captain's, and I told him so, right then and there."

Tim leaned forward in his chair and asked eagerly, "What did he say?"

"He told me I was in luck, because anyone could be a master and commander. But in the same breath he warned me that only a few ever make it."

"How come? Why do only a few make it?"

Peter calmly said, "Because they won't follow the Master and Commander Code."

"What code?!" Tim exclaimed, nearly falling out of his chair.

Peter sat back and smiled while he looked back at the young captain and saw himself some thirty years before, eagerly asking the same question.

"Tim, now calm down, sit back, and listen. I'll tell you the code, but only on one condition."

Tim could hardly control his emotions and interrupted the master and commander (for this, he now knew, was what Captain Peter truly was) for the third time in under a minute. "Name it! What's the condition? I want to know the code; I want to be a master and commander, too!"

"I believe you, I believe you," Peter repeated as he slowly leaned forward and looked directly into Tim's eyes without blinking. The master and commander's intensity startled Tim. He had the feeling Peter was trying to look directly into his soul.

Peter spoke slowly and distinctly. "The one condition is very simple. I'll teach you the code only if you tell me what you're willing to give up to follow the code."

This took Tim by surprise. "What do you mean, what I'd be willing to give up? What kinds of things do I have to give up?"

"For one, most of your friends. You won't lose all your friends, just the ones that aren't your true friends. You'll be lonely quite a bit, you'll feel lost, get scared, be bone tired, doubt yourself. You might even cry yourself to sleep once or twice. You'll fail many more times than you'll succeed, and sometimes you won't even know when you've succeeded. The code isn't for everyone; not everyone wants to be a master and commander enough to become one."

Considering what had happened to Tim that day, and all the quips he'd received from his so-called friend Ted, he didn't think losing his friends would be hard, but the seriousness of Peter's tone made him think twice before replying. "I . . . I . . . I want to know the code, Peter," Tim said slowly.

"Okay, fair enough. Then tell me what you're willing to sacrifice to be in charge of your course, to be a master and commander? How important is it to you, really? Is it a nice-to-have or is it a must-come –to-be in your life?"

Before Tim could answer, the wily captain continued with his questioning. "These are big questions Tim, and I don't expect you to give me your answer tonight. You need to sleep on this, really think about what it would feel like to chart your own course, to leave a perfectly safe harbor for a land you're not sure exists. Imagine what it's like to be at sea and not see land, how scared you would be knowing that no one could help you. But then imagine the joy of finding a new harbor and learning new skills that will help you find even more harbors. What would you do with the knowledge and courage to go anywhere and do anything that matters to you?"

Tim's mind raced. He'd never thought like this before. He could feel his heart beating faster as he imagined charting his own courses around the globe. Where would he go first? What kind of improvements would he make to his ship? What about all the money he'd make; what would he spend it on? As his mind darted from one day-dream to the next, Peter brought Tim back to reality.

"Tim, tonight I'll tell you a couple of my sea stories and about the life I've encountered outside Hardwork Harbor. Then, if you wake up in the morning as excited as you are now, if you've put some meaningful thought behind what you're willing to sacrifice to become a master and commander, and if you're willing to share those thoughts with me, I'll welcome you aboard the *Persistence* and share the code with you. Sound fair?"

Tim almost didn't hear the question. He sat there staring back at Peter as if he was truly seeing him for the first time. He couldn't believe what he was hearing. He nodded rapidly before he could get any words out, as if afraid the master and commander would change his offer before Tim could respond.

As Peter smiled back at Tim, Jack bounded around the counter to personally serve the master and commander and the first-timer their chowder and fried clams. "Okay, sailors, take it slow and savor every bite. It doesn't get any better than this!" beamed Jack as he delivered two bowls of piping-hot, chunky, creamy clam chowder and two heaping plates full of golden-fried full-belly clams served on top of thinly sliced French fries and coleslaw. Jack placed a bottle of his own branded malt vinegar between them and stated, "Use this to your heart's content. Enjoy, boys!"

They could barely get the words "Thank you, Jack" out of their mouths before their attention turned to tasting Jack's creations. After a few minutes of silent savoring, Peter began to tell the young captain some of his sea stories. Tim heard about how the Persistence almost sank when it encountered ice in the Northwest Passage, and how Peter spent a winter in a harbor run by a village of Eskimos who helped weld steel plates to the bow of the Persistence so he could navigate the icy waters undaunted.

Then there was the story of how Captain Peter journeyed to Africa to deliver food and medicine to a starving nation, only to learn that there were no piers to off-load the cargo the villagers so desperately needed. Peter figured out a way to move an anchor and a motorized winch to the stern of the *Persistence* and *purposely* ran his ship bow-first onto the beach to off-load the food and medicine. His stern-powered anchor invention then pulled his vessel off the beach and, because his stern was in deeper water, his propellers were never damaged.

His final story of the evening was about taking cargo halfway around the world, a job only the largest ships could do because of the need to carry such large quantities of fuel. Peter had worked with engineers to design and create a battery system that would recharge from his main engines so he could go longer with less fuel, thus enabling him to win business against the larger fleets.

Tim was riveted by these stories of invention, resourcefulness, and excitement. Oh, how he'd love to know what it felt like to conquer the northern seas or help a village of sick and starving people or beat the big guys by being smarter. He was so enthralled with the stories that Peter had to remind him that if he didn't finish what was on his plate, Jack would not be happy.

As the meal came to an end, Tim longed for more stories, but Captain Peter hinted to Tim that he'd have to wait until tomorrow. They said thank you to Jack and congratulated him on creating the perfect clam chowder and fried clams. As they waved goodbye to the chef, Peter confirmed his commitment to meet with Jack the following afternoon.

When they reached the gangway of the *Persistence*, Peter said, "Okay, Tim, you've got the helm; you decide the next course. If you're willing to tell me what you'd give up to learn the code, then I'll see you soon. If not, it was a pleasure dining with you this evening, and I wish you all the best on your career as a captain." Tim had so much he wanted to ask Peter, but he could tell from the skipper's tone that tonight wasn't the night; it was time for Tim to do some serious thinking before he could earn time with this remarkable man. As Peter shook his hand to say goodnight, Tim was able to ask one more question."I read you loud and clear, Skipper. Thank you. Thank you for a wonderful evening." Tim paused for a moment and continued, "By the way, I'm curious, what did all those nicknames Jack called you mean?"

Peter released Tim's hand, smiled as he turned to the gangplank, and said as he was looking over his shoulder, "Persistent Pete." He gave Tim a wink, turned, and headed to his quarters on the *Persistence*.

Tim stood there and quietly repeated Peter's nickname. There was so much Tim could learn from this man; he didn't want to leave. He knew he wanted to learn the code, and he wanted to shout back to Persistent Pete that he would be back the next day, but he didn't want to sound so automatic. He wanted the skipper to know he was going to take the question seriously. This also gave Tim a slightly uneasy feeling. The captain was intense. Could Tim really be like him? Could he convince the master and commander to teach him the code?

T im didn't sleep well that night. He desperately
wanted to formulate the perfect answer for Captain Peter so he could
learn the Master and Commander Code. But all he could come up
with was his willingness to give up trying to hang out with Ted.

Tim kept repeating the question out loud: "What am I willing to
give up? What will I sacrifice to learn the code?"

Then he thought about the captain's earlier remark: "Understand
the 'why' and you'll figure out the 'way.' "

Tim was stuck. He wanted to learn the code, but at what cost he
didn't really know. Then he started thinking about what it would be
like to travel the world, to do the things he wanted to do, to help the
people he could help, to see new places and learn new things. He
started thinking about his life in a new way. He was no longer imag-
ining a life in which work alternated with play. What if he no longer

Action #1
Understand
the Why

worked to live; what if he lived to work? What if work was no longer just a job, but something more, with a purpose greater than a paycheck? What if his work could make a difference in the world? What would he be willing to give up to live a life with purpose?

In the early morning, as the sun came up and turned the still waters around his boat into a golden mirror, a thought hit Tim: The captain wanted him to understand his "why." If Tim could understand his "why," the captain would help him understand the way!

As Tim watched bubbles from the maintenance crew ripple the golden surface of the water he paced his decks, thinking about his why. He'd never thought like this before. School had taught him how to do things right, but not how to do the thing that was right for himself. University had prepared him to serve in a larger organization, to follow the rules and do the right things to get a job done. But what the master and commander was saying was completely different, incredibly exciting yet also terrifying: he was asking if Tim was willing to live his dreams.

Tim started to question himself. Did he really want the master and commander's way of life? Did he want to live a life with a risky outcome? All the captains in the fleet knew that if they worked hard and delivered the goods, they'd be well paid over time and could then retire and cruise the coastal waterways. But Peter hadn't taken that path. He'd chosen to leave the security of the fleet behind and follow his own course. Could Tim do this? Could he choose his own course? Doubt entered his mind as fatigue crept up on him. How could he possibly navigate the high seas when he hadn't even been able to navigate the bay the day before?

As these thoughts swirled through his mind, he watched a barge passing by, pulled by a tug. He saw the captain of the barge sitting in his captain's chair at the helm and reading a newspaper. The captain clearly didn't care where his barge was being towed—and why should he? He couldn't steer it anyhow. "I guess I'd read the newspaper, too, if my boat was a barge," Tim muttered to himself.

The barge captain

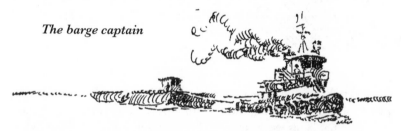

That got Tim thinking that the barge captain was helping another captain fulfill *his* dreams. The barge captain was working because he had to, not because he wanted to. He was helping another captain do what he *wanted* to do. The barge captain wasn't getting to follow his dream, unless his dream was to be a barge captain. But Tim thought that couldn't be the case. Why would anyone want to spend the rest of his life being towed around and told what to do?

At that very moment Tim's mind changed course. He didn't want to live his life helping other captains fulfill their dreams. He wanted to chart his own course. He wanted to go after his own dreams, and he was willing to sacrifice everything to live that kind of life. He'd risk it all because, the way he figured it, he only had one life to live, so why not live the life he wanted? Tim had a contented look on his face as he saluted the barge captain, as if to say, "Thanks for helping me understand my 'why.'" Later that day, after a quick nap to refresh himself, Tim paced the pier in front of the mighty *Persistence*. He marveled at her as she glistened under the glow of the late-day sun. She was a boat built with purpose, and now that he understood the reasoning behind some of her modifications, like her double-thick bow and massive stern anchor, he admired her even more. Tim was wondering what other modifications the master and commander had made to the *Persistence* when he felt the firm grip of a strong hand squeeze his shoulder.

Startled, Tim turned to find Captain Peter dressed in a wetsuit dripping with salt water, a scuba tank attached to his back. It took a moment for Tim to recognize the master and commander; he hadn't expected to see him in a diving gear!

"Ah, Captain Peter?" Tim asked.

"The one and the only, Tim, and stop calling me captain," Peter said with a wink.

Regaining his composure, Tim asked, "Are you a diver too?" He was perplexed. He had never heard of a captain learning to scuba dive, let alone one diving in the murky waters of Hardwork Harbor.

"I'm verifying the work that was just completed on the *Persistence*," Peter said calmly as he dropped his fins onto the pier and began to take off his scuba tank. "The reason I'm visiting Hardwork Harbor is to swap out my propellers for these new ones that were just invented. I've read about how they improve performance by creating less drag in the water. They're supposed to be the next big breakthrough in propulsion technology, so I figured they were worth testing. My attitude is, 'If you're not improving your ship, then you're not improving, and when you stop improving, you start slowing down.' And I'm not ready to slow down, Tim — you tracking with me?"

Tim remained quiet and nodded slowly as he focused on committing Peter's words to memory.

"But still, I don't get the scuba gear. There are plenty of skilled divers around here. Why are you diving?" Tim was perplexed. He watched as the master and commander gently laid the scuba tank on the deck next to his fins.

"A wise captain once told me to 'trust, but verify.' I trust the captains of this propeller company to do a great job — that's why I'm here — but these propellers are critical to my boat. If they don't work, I'm dead in the water. I want to learn everything I can about them and, more importantly, I want to learn how to fix them if and when something goes wrong — like hitting a sandbar." Peter smirked and poked Tim in the ribs.

Tim forced a half-laugh at the comment and looked back at his boat, where the dive crew was surfacing. He wondered if he should jump in the water with a mask and inspect their work.

He was thinking about where to find a mask, since he didn't have one onboard let alone know how to scuba dive, when Peter broke in with a question: "Well, I assume you're not here to watch me get out of my diving gear. What can I do for you, Tim?"

"I... I'd like to learn the code, Peter," Tim stuttered, finally getting the answer out. "I've thought long and hard about it and I want to learn it."

Peter nodded slowly and gave Tim another of his laser-like stares, then said, "Are you ready to tell me what you're willing to give up in order to learn the code?"

"Yes, I am," Tim responded, as his back stiffened.

"Excellent!" exclaimed Peter. "Come aboard and make yourself comfortable in the wardroom. I'll be there directly." With that, Peter motioned Tim to follow him aboard while he carried his gear to the dive locker in *Persistence*'s stern.

Captain Peter returned to the galley only a few minutes later, but that was more than enough time for Tim's hands to go from clammy to dripping with sweat as he prepared his thoughts for the master and commander.

Peter entered the wardroom with the energy of a captain half his age. Tim watched how his heels barely touched the floor; he seemed to be walking only on the balls of his feet. The young captain hadn't noticed this before, but Peter was in remarkably good shape for someone who was thirty years older than himself.

Peter broke the silence with a broad grin and said with excitement, "So tell me what's on your mind, Tim."

Tim's response came slowly at first; he wanted to deliver the right answer to Peter's question. "Well, I've thought a lot about what you said to me last night, and I'm certain that I want to be a master and commander. I want to help people as you do, and travel the world and make improvements to my ship, just like you, and I want to..." Tim had thought he could win Peter over by praising his accomplishments, but Peter raised his hand as if to signal a halt. Tim went quiet in midsentence.

"Tim, this isn't about doing what I've done; this is about doing what you want to do. This is about charting your own courses and having the courage to steer them. That's what the code is all about." Peter paused for a moment for the words to sink in. "Look, everyone wants to have a nice ship or great experience or lots of money, but not everyone is willing to work for it—really work for it. Not everyone appreciates that it's not about what harbor you land in, it's about the course you took to get there." Peter paused and leaned forward with even more intensity than he had displayed the previous night. "Now tell me, Tim, have you thought about what you're willing to give up in order to follow your own course?"

Tim blinked several times, taken aback by the captain's sudden intensity. "Yes...yes, I have, sir," he stuttered.

Peter disregarded the "sir" but sat upright in his chair, as if he couldn't wait to hear Tim's answer. "Okay, tell me," he said, in a tone that sounded more like an order than a request.

"I...I...I'd dedicate my life to following the code."

Peter squinted at Tim as if sighting him with a rifle scope, then slowly leaned back in his chair before asking, "What do you mean by that?"

Tim fidgeted on the edge of his seat while rubbing his hands together nervously. He looked around the galley, took a deep breath, and then let his emotions answer the question. "Last night you talked to me about understanding the 'why,' and you said if I understood the why then I'd figure out the way."

"Yes, yes, please keep going," Peter said, calmly but with encouragement.

"That got me to thinking about what course in life I want to take, and how I have one life in which to chart those courses, so why not chart the courses that matter most to me."

Peter was getting more excited, his eyes wide and a grin growing as he leaned forward in an effort to encourage the young sea captain to keep talking. Tim picked up on Peter's excitement and started talking with more confidence, from his heart.

"And as I spent all night trying to figure out the right answer to your question, I realized there is no one right answer, only the right answer for me, and that answer is understanding the 'why' behind why I want to learn the code to becoming a master and commander. And that if I understand the 'why,' you might help me figure out the 'way.'"

Peter spoke slowly as he asked his next question. "And what did you come to understand about your 'why?'"

Tim took another deep breath and responded. "I realized today, as I watched a captain who had been given a boat just like mine many years ago, that he'd let his boat be turned into a barge and now spends his days following someone else's course. I don't want that course, Peter. I don't want to feel like I have to go to work to live; instead I want to live to work. I want to be excited about the course I'm on. I want to have purpose. I want my life to mean something." Peter smiled, nodding repeatedly, as Tim spoke. Tim took one more deep breath and concluded, "And I'm willing to spend the rest of my life following courses that inspire me. The way I figure it, that's a life worth living, and I'm willing to risk it all for that kind of life."

Peter jumped to his feet, leaped across the room, grabbed Tim by his shoulders, and shouted, "That's what I'm talking about, Tim! That's what life is all about; having the courage to follow your own courses!"

Tim had to tighten his stomach muscles to absorb the excited shoulder-shaking he was receiving from Peter. He was surprised how strong this elder captain was, but more important, he was relieved that the risk he had taken, speaking from his heart, was exactly what Peter had been looking for. And before Tim could ask the question, Peter said the words that made him beam. "It would be my honor to share with you the code for becoming a master and commander!" Peter exclaimed. "Before I do, however, we need to discuss a few things. First of all, there are eight actions that define the Master and Commander Code. I use the term 'actions' because an action is what's required to make anything happen. I'll tell you about the eight actions, but...." And here Peter paused, even as Tim regained the composure he had lost under the onslaught of the elder captain's excitement. "Before I do," Peter said then, "I have another question to ask you." Tim responded with a slow, cautious nod.

"Tim, do you know how to dream?"

This caught the young captain completely off guard, and he had to ask the older captain to repeat the question so he could gather his thoughts on how to answer it.

"Huh? What did you say?"

Peter didn't pause. "Do you know how to dream?" Before Tim could answer, Peter offered him a reprieve, saying, "You know, don't you, that most people don't know how to dream. It's nothing to be ashamed of; most folks just let their minds run wild on whatever lights their fancy at a particular moment."

Tim still wasn't tracking with the captain, so he tossed off a half-answer, partly in the hope of clarification and partly to stall for time: "I thought dreaming is what your mind does when you're asleep," he said sheepishly.

"Oh yes," said Peter, "that is a form of dreaming, but what I'm talking about is enabling your mind to dream about the things you want it to dream about."

Tim was still bewildered. He'd certainly daydreamed about things from time to time — normal stuff, like a beautiful woman or a bigger boat or beating Ted on a cargo route. But surely this was not what the master and commander was referring to. As Tim tried to find the words to answer Peter's seemingly simple question, Peter interrupted the awkward silence.

"To become a master and commander, you first need to know how to dream. You can't put the code to work without a dream to follow. And to dream *big* dreams, to dream dreams that *Fire YOU UP*, you need to learn how, and the bigger the dreams the better."

Tim didn't know what to say. No one had ever asked him to dream before; the last time he had had any serious conversations about his dreams was when his parents would comfort him after a nightmare. Tim fidgeted in his chair, again replying only with a nod of his head.

"The problem is, Tim, most people don't allow themselves time to dream. They don't ask the 'what' questions. Great dreams come from great questions. The better the questions, the more exciting your dreams!" Peter said with enthusiasm.

"Ah, okay, like what kind of questions?" Tim asked, a hint of skepticism in his voice.

The senior captain sensed Tim's apprehension and changed tacks. "Okay, look Tim, I know this sounds a bit farfetched, but how do you think I came up with the idea to steam the Northwest Passage, or take critical supplies to that tribe in Africa, or create a fuel-saving system to cross the Pacific?" Peter paused for effect, then added, "I wasn't born with these ideas. I didn't come pre-programmed with these courses to pursue. I dreamed them up, and I started by asking the question, 'What would I do if I knew I couldn't fail?' " Peter didn't pause to allow Tim time to interrupt. "Think about that question, Tim. I mean really think about it, without any limitations. That's harder to do than you might think, because whether you like it or not, your brain has already come to accept limitations that have been imposed by other people."

Peter continued without pause, "One of the most important elements in dreaming is to dream without limitations, to dream with reckless abandon, to dream as if no one is watching or judging you. Dreaming is very personal — it's what makes you, you. But to dream big dreams, you have to dream without limits, and that can be hard when you've grown up learning the rules of your house, the rules at school, the rules at work."

Tim's eyes were starting to light up; his eyebrows were starting to rise. Peter could see from Tim's body language that he was starting to catch on. "Tim, remember this. It's an important fact, a fact to live by," the master and commander said as he got up from his captain's chair and grabbed a black pen and notepad from a neighboring nightstand. Handing the note-taking tools to Tim, he said his next words very slowly. "You have only two limitations in life. Number one"—and here Peter held up his index finger to make his point clear—"your imagination. And number two, your determination."

Peter paused as he watched Tim mouth the words to himself while frantically scribbling them down on the notepad. The master and commander stiffened, his voice becoming stern with conviction as he leveled his gaze directly into Tim's eyes. "No one, and I mean *no one*, decides your limitations. You and *you alone* decide what you can or can't do. Do you understand this concept? Don't accept a limitation unless you've proven to yourself that it's your own limitation, and even then you don't have to accept it." The older captain maintained a slow but stern tone as he repeated himself to ensure that Tim grasped the full extent of his point. "Too many young and impressionable captains accept someone else's limitations as their own. Just because someone else says you can't do something, doesn't mean you can't. You alone must decide whether you can or can't do it. One of my favorite sayings is, 'Whether you think you can or, you think you can't — you're right.' "

Peter paused again as he watched Tim close his eyes and whisper the words aloud. "Whether you think you can or, you think you can't — you're right." Tim said softly, as he once again feverishly committed the captain's words to paper.

"You see, dreaming and limitations go hand in hand. If you believe you have limitations, your dreams will be circumscribed by those limitations and you'll never enable yourself to dream bigger."

A light bulb went off in Tim's head, and he nearly shouted as he interrupted his seafaring teacher, "But wait! How do I know which limitations I've accepted aren't really my limitations?"

Peter smiled. His student was listening. "You won't know until you ask more questions of yourself."

Tim responded, "Like what?"

"Not 'like what,' " the master and commander replied, "but 'what if.' "

"Ah, I'm not sure I'm following you," Tim said. These questions within questions were making his head spin.

"Tim, as you dream up answers to the question 'what would I do if I knew I couldn't fail,' keep asking yourself 'what if?' When I was dreaming up ways to compete against the large fleets for routes that are halfway around the world, I kept getting stuck on the fact that my ship didn't have a fuel tank large enough to handle those routes. It was only after I started dreaming about what-if scenarios that I dreamed up the idea of using batteries to help extend my range."

Peter continued. "Now the battery idea wasn't my first idea; I dreamt about ways to harness the wind to help me accomplish this dream. I started by dreaming about sails. Then I realized I would need a mast and boom and a deeper keel. These sounded like too many modifications, so then I dreamt about creating a massive kite-boarding sail that didn't require a mast, and so on and so on, until I finally settled on charting a course to develop a battery system that would give me the range I needed."

Tim was starting to understand the method to the master's dreaming madness, and he smiled slowly as he nodded his head in agreement.

"These dreams didn't happen overnight. It took time and focus to dream up this idea, and then it took even longer to make the dream come true."

Tim interjected excitedly, "But you did it! You invented a system that helped you beat the big guys!"

"You're right, I did, but that's not what drove me to invent it. It's true I was trying to figure out a way to compete against the big fleets, but my 'why' for investing the time, effort, and money to build the system came from my realization that if I didn't create this system, I would never get the opportunity to explore certain regions of the world. And the more I thought about that limitation, the more I realized that I didn't want that as a limitation in my life."

Tim jumped to his feet and exclaimed, "That was your 'why,' and creating the battery system was you figuring out your way!"

A broad smile lifted across the older sea captain's face. Without realizing it, Tim had just learned the first action of the Master and Commander Code: UNDERSTAND YOUR WHY, AND YOU'LL FIGURE OUT THE WAY.

Tim was beaming; he had caught the elder captain's drift. The 'why,' the purpose of his dream, was the starting point to create a course of action. His mind was buzzing with ideas. He couldn't wait to start dreaming up answers to the question of what he would do if he knew he couldn't fail. As if on cue, Peter interrupted Tim's train of thought and said encouragingly, "That's exactly correct, Tim. Congratulations, you've just learned the first action to becoming a master and commander: Understand your why, and you'll figure out the way." Peter repeated the action calmly and then continued, "This is the

Captain Peter

single most important first step in making any dream come true. You must understand the importance of the dream to you. Dig into the 'why' behind your dream. Ask yourself why you should commit your most precious resource to pursuing your dream."

Tim sat down slowly as he looked at Peter, tilted his headed slightly to one side, and asked, "What's my most precious resource?"

"Time," Peter responded, pausing briefly for effect. "Time, Tim. Each of us has only so much time to live, and how you spend your time is totally up to you. But once you use your time, you can't get it back, so make it count — every minute of it. I'm not saying you shouldn't take time to play and have fun; what I'm saying is that you should be aware what you're spending your time on. You wouldn't believe what you can get done if you manage your time well. The bigger the dream you go after, the more time you'll need to make it come true."

"Got it. I'm tracking with you, Peter," Tim said, as he hurried to take notes. Then he asked, "So what's Action #2?"

Peter leaned forward for effect. "Tim, before we get to the next action, it's important that you understand Action #1."

Tim shot back a high-energy look and exclaimed, "I got it. I got it, really. Understand my why, and I'll figure out the way."

The salty sea captain wasn't buying Tim's exuberant response, and he ratcheted up his tone a bit to ensure that Tim understood the seriousness of Action #1. "Tim, this is *much* easier to say than it is to do, and unfortunately, the only way to understand the importance of this action is to experience it. The first time I left the harbor, I thought I understood my 'why.' I wanted to earn enough money to paint my ship a new color and get some nice shiny stainless steel cleats and exhaust stacks, and I wrongly thought that my 'why' for leaving the harbor was strong enough to keep me going when the winds and waves were against me. Tim, I didn't even make it past the breakwater. Waves pummeled my bow, and water started filling my bilges faster than my pumps could drain them. I was sinking, and all I could think about was how quickly I could get back into the harbor."

Peter waited as his words sank in, then continued. "I panicked, and realized that sinking wasn't worth a few new fixtures on my boat. I tried to turn around in the middle of the channel and only made my situation worse as the waves pounded my boat broadside."

Tim stared at the captain in disbelief. He couldn't imagine encountering waves that big. He asked, "What did you do?"

"I did the only thing I could at that moment. I was about to sink — I was going to lose my ship — so I powered up the engine and ran my boat aground."

Tim was shell-shocked by Captain Peter's confession. He couldn't believe the master had purposely run his boat aground. Doing so must have been incredibly difficult, but it had been Peter's last option before the unthinkable occurred. Tim shuddered at the thought.

While Tim was still grasping the captain's story, Peter went on to explain the importance of understanding the true value of your "why."

"I sat out there overnight getting hammered constantly by waves. I didn't sleep a wink, lost all my gear that wasn't tied down, which was pretty much everything, and didn't even have a line to offer the rescue tugs when they arrived at slack tide the next morning. I was a mess."

Tim asked quietly, "What did you do next? What happened to your boat?"

"I spent the next six months licking my wounds, hearing from everyone in the harbor how stupid my stunt had been. Worse still, I started to believe what the others were telling me. I found myself thinking about a life working the local routes inside Hardwork Harbor. I got pretty good at convincing myself that I could have a nice life working my way up the ranks in one of those fleets. I had almost convinced myself and my friends that I would never attempt another 'crazy' course outside the harbor when I met a master and commander, and he shared with me the things I'm sharing now with you."

Peter stood up and walked to the galley for drinks as he spoke matter-of-factly about his near-death experience and never wanting to leave the harbor again. He raised his voice slightly to continue his conversation with Tim as he prepared two glasses of ice water.

"You know one of the first things that master and commander said to me?" Peter asked. "He said, 'Son, never leave the harbor without a *why* worth dying for.' "

Peter went silent as he watched Tim's jaw drop upon hearing those words. "He, he told you that?" Tim asked. "A 'why' worth dying for?"

The wily captain merely nodded to allow the seriousness of the words to linger a few moments longer.

"Ah, Peter, I'm not looking to die anytime soon. What exactly did that master and commander mean by a 'why' worth dying for?" Tim asked sheepishly.

Peter handed the young captain a glass of water, looked dead-center into his eyes, and said as he lowered himself back into his chair, "What he meant was, establish a why that you're willing to sacrifice everything to go after. He wasn't asking me to set a suicide course — far from it. He was driving home the point that most people think they know why they want to do something, but they give up way before they accomplish their dream."

Peter took a quick sip of water so as not to give Tim a chance to ask another question, then continued. "What he wanted me to learn is that most people don't have a strong enough reason — a strong enough 'why' — to stick with their course when the going gets tough. Case in point, I hadn't even left the breakwater of Hardwork Harbor when I determined that my original 'why' of wanting shiny new hardware for my boat wasn't worth sinking for. This master and commander had served in a military fleet before navigating his own courses around the world, and had been put in situations that made him ask himself if the course the military wanted him to steer was worth dying for, which is how he came to define a valid 'why' as one that is worth dying for."

Peter paused briefly and studied Tim's body language to ensure that what he was saying was registering. "You know, it's an interesting question and one that I've asked myself many times over the course of my life."

Tim barely let the older captain finish. "What question? What did you ask yourself?"

"What do I feel so strongly about that I'm willing to die trying to accomplish it?" Peter said matter-of-factly.

"Oh, that question. I've never thought of asking myself that," Tim mumbled, as he looked down at his notes, not wanting even to say the word "die."

Picking up on Tim's discomfort, Peter responded in a reassuring tone. "Tim, relax. No one is asking you to die for your 'why.' I'm just trying to help you build a frame of reference for finding a 'why' that's powerful enough to help you stick it out when your course gets tough — and trust me, any course worth following will get tough, and there will come a time when you will ask yourself the next question."

The young captain perked up with some semblance of relief and asked, "What question is that?"

"When the waves are crashing over your bow, the wind is blowing you off course, the currents are pushing you backward, and you haven't slept in days, you *will* ask yourself, 'Is this course worth steering?' Is all the struggle and hard work worth it? At first you won't pay much attention to it, but as your course becomes harder, doubt will inevitably creep into your mind and attempt to convince you to turn around, to turn away from your challenging course and set a course instead to a safe harbor, one that will shield you from the turbulent seas you're facing at that very instant." Tim nodded with wide eyes as he tried to imagine a sea state like the one the captain was describing. "When doubt comes knocking, you need to be prepared to knock it back, and the best way to knock it back is to understand your 'why.' You with me, Tim?"

"Oh, I'm understanding you, Peter." Tim took a deeper breath as if to say, "I get your drift, Cap'n," and wrote a quick fragment on his notepad: *Beat doubt back by building stronger whys.*

"Good, because I can't stress this rule enough. Don't ever go to sea without understanding your 'why.' I've seen good captains sink because they went to sea for the wrong reasons, and the saddest part was that they had what it took to become a master and commander, but they didn't understand their why. If they had, they would have learned about Action #2."

Tim sat bolt upright, eagerly awaiting the next action for becoming a master and commander, and responded excitedly to Peter's remark. "What's that — what's Action #2?"

But Peter offered only one word. "Plan," he said.

HOW TO GET STARTED

Action #1: Understand Your *Why*

All these years later, I can hear the pulmonary doctor's words as if it were yesterday: "Mrs. Mills, I recommend that your son learn the game of chess."

Those aren't words most twelve-year-olds want to hear, especially a twelve-year-old who loved hunting snakes, frogs, and turtles, riding his bike, and exploring the great outdoors. My eyes started to fill with tears as I tried to imagine giving up all that. Thankfully, my mom had me leave the room before the doctor could finish his prognosis of the severity of my asthma. I sat in the waiting room, crying quietly. The more I thought about each thing I'd never do again, the more I cried.

Once again, though, Mom came to my rescue. When she found me crying, she dug her fingernails into my forearm, saying, "Alden, look at me and remember these words: No one, and I mean NO ONE, decides what you can or can't do. You decide — no one else."

Then and there, my mom taught me the essence of Action #1: Understand what you want to do, then do it. She set me on a new course that day, one that would include overcoming asthma, leading U.S. Navy SEALs, and building companies. Of course, at the ripe old age of twelve I couldn't fully grasp what she was trying to teach me: that my life was up to me — not the asthma doctor, not a teacher, not a classmate, but me.

It's a pretty simple concept when you think about it. Each of us decides what he or she can or can't do. No one else makes that decision for us. It gets a little harder, however, when you're going after something that you're not sure you can achieve—which is probably true of any dream that's really worth pursuing. I compiled a list of compelling reasons why it was critically important to make it through Navy SEAL training, but as convincing as those reasons were, I grappled with internal demons of doubt—not to mention the demonic doubt the SEAL instructors infused throughout the training. Those demons of doubt were no different from the ones that reared their ugly heads when I was starting the Perfect Fitness Company. In that case the self-doubt crept into my mind when we ran out of money, and the SEAL instructors were replaced with impatient investors who asked why I wouldn't give up and get a real job. Six months before Perfect Fitness launched, one investor said to me, "Alden, it's over. Go get a real job. You are starting to embarrass yourself."

Conquering asthma, becoming a Navy SEAL, and launching a company were personal goals. Though each goal was different, the fundamental actions required to accomplish each one were *exactly* the same. They all started with a clear understanding of what I wanted to accomplish and why. Here are a few examples:

• *Conquering asthma:* The idea that I couldn't go outside to play with friends, explore the woods, and ride my bike was intolerable. I decided I'd rather be sick for life than give up the things that made me happy.

• *Becoming a Navy SEAL:* As a Naval Academy graduate, I had made a five-year service commitment to my country. I *love* the water, team sports, and being outside, but the thought of spending the next five years in a submarine or a ship's engine room was horrifying. I was willing to suffer heavily to avoid five years of confinement. (Ironically, I would go on to lead two mini-sub SEAL platoons and spent many months on submarines, only to learn that it wasn't as bad as I had imagined.)

• *Launching a company:* I could not resign myself to a career spent climbing a corporate ladder, with someone else dictating how much vacation time I could have or how much I would be paid. Also, I wanted to be able to look my children in the eyes someday and tell them that they could do anything they decided they could do — and how could I tell them that without first doing it myself?

All three of these examples represent what I call Milestone Goals — goals that took me years to accomplish and became milestones, or life-changing accomplishments, in my life. You attain a Milestone Goal by achieving a series of Pebble Goals. For instance, to get accepted to SEAL

Training, I needed to do 120 push-ups, 100 sit-ups, and 20 pull-ups (not to mention a 1.5-mile run and an 800-yard swim). None of these was easy for me; each one became a Pebble Goal. Intermediate goals are important components in any accomplishment, but the trick is learning how not to give up on your journey toward the ultimate destination, the Milestone Goal. How do you build this unstoppable persistence?

It all starts with understanding your "why" — your reason for going after your goal. Knowing the reason behind your goal is the fuel that will keep you going when everyone else tells you to quit. Your why will give you the power to push back the demons of doubt that will inevitably creep into your mind (and trust me, they will). Understanding your why is your perseverance engine — it keeps you going even when you think you can't. It's that important. Know your why before you start the journey!

So how do you get to understanding your why? What's worked for me is using what I call my Outcome Accounts. Whenever I dream up a new Milestone Goal, I create an Outcome Account. It's a simple way to test how truly important this goal is to me. Some goals are just not as important as others — some are just nice-to-have goals, not must-haves. You can use Outcome Accounts for any goal, but I find this tool especially helpful when I'm going after a Milestone Goal — something that will require months, if not years, of persistence to attain.

Here's how an Outcome Account works:

• At the top of a sheet of paper, identify and underline your goal. Example: <u>I want to graduate from the Naval Academy.</u>

• Beneath your underlined goal, divide the paper into left and right halves with a vertical line down the center.

• Place a plus sign (+) at the top of the left column and a minus sign (-) at the top of the right column.

• In the plus column, list every positive outcome of achieving this goal. For example, my graduation from the Naval Academy would mean:

• I would be the first person in my family to accomplish this goal;

• I would be able to serve as an officer in the Navy;

• I would have a chance of becoming a Navy SEAL platoon commander;

Outcome Account
GOAL

(+)	(-)

• I would do things few people in the country ever get to do;

• I would graduate from a place many people said I couldn't graduate from, including a few teachers and company officers who worked there!

• In the minus column, list every negative outcome of NOT achieving this goal. For example, if I were NOT to graduate from the Naval Academy:

• It would mean I would have to serve in the Navy as an enlisted man in the deck division on a ship to pay back the time I had spent at the Academy;

• It would mean that every person who said I couldn't graduate was right. I'd have to hear their smug voices and see their smirks as they said "I told you so";

• It would take me a lot longer to earn a commission as a naval officer and even longer to earn an opportunity to become a Navy SEAL platoon commander;

• It would mean I had failed at something I believed I could do;

• It would mean I hadn't tried hard enough — I would have let myself down due to laziness and taking the easy way out.

These pluses and minuses helped me understand why I wanted to stay at the Naval Academy and commit to graduating. There was a time at the end of my sophomore year when I considered leaving the Naval Academy, but I found my determination to stay in *both* columns: the positives of graduating and the negatives of failing to graduate. Both the pluses and the minuses inspired me to persevere when many people at the academy said I couldn't do it. It didn't help that I had already received the maximum demerits for a senior by the end of my sophomore year. To graduate, I needed to avoid getting another demerit for two entire years! No wonder my company officer said I would never make it.

But I did make it, and I did so using some of the very examples I listed above as my inspiration to keep going when everyone else said "There's NO WAY you're gonna graduate, Midshipman Mills." My Outcome Account kept me going. As in Freud's Psychology of Human Behavior— Avoiding Pain and Seeking Pleasure — I had unknowingly created great inspiration from my negative outcome column, not wanting to give others the satisfaction of knowing what I could or couldn't do better than I did. That turned into my single biggest motivating factor in sticking with it day after day for those next two years.

Over time I have found myself creating Outcome Accounts in my head. I'll list a whole series of pluses and minuses of the desired outcome, and when I come across a plus or a minus that hits me at gut level and gets me daydreaming about what it would feel like to accomplish a particular goal, I know I've discovered the "why" behind what I want to go after. At the Naval Academy, I would go to sleep thinking about those individuals who said I couldn't graduate; I would hear their voices, I would see their faces. No detail was too small for me — I visualized every element of the day that I would graduate and what it would feel like if and when I ever saw those doubters again. I didn't realize it at the time, but I was personalizing my goal and visualizing its outcome. The more I did it, the more it inspired me to keep going.

For every goal since then, I've used an Outcome Account to outline my reason for putting my head down, working hard, and filtering out those who will help me from those who want to see me fail. The Outcome Account is my single most important first step toward being UNSTOPPABLE. As Master and Commander Peter teaches young Captain Tim, "Once you understand your why, you'll figure out your way."

Tim sat across from the weathered captain with a bewildered look on his face and said, "Action #2 is to plan? That's it?"

"Yep, that's it. First you understand, then you plan," Peter said with a smile.

"Ah, okay — got it — understand, then plan. What's Action #3?" Tim said as if he were repeating a math equation in a classroom. He felt certain that Action #3 would be more interesting than Action #2.

"I'll tell you Action #3 right after you tell me about the plan you made to cross the bay yesterday," Peter said, a little smile creeping up the right side of his tanned face.

"Uh, well, I, ah, I didn't write the plan down. I just followed my normal route until I reached Daymarker #7 and turned to course zero-one-zero." Tim struggled to organize his thoughts while trying to remember a course he had spent the last twenty-four hours trying to forget.

Action #2
Plan in 3-D

Peter prodded Tim. "Huh. So you didn't write down a new course. How come?"

"I...I...." Tim paused, then sighed, as if to say "You got me," and confessed, "I didn't write the plan down because I didn't think it was important. I had traveled the portion of the course for the last year and knew it like the back of my hand. I didn't think the new course would be that hard." Tim's shoulders dropped forward as a dejected look spread across his face.

Peter didn't allow Tim's dejected thoughts to linger. He responded quickly, "Of course you didn't; any young captain would have done the same thing. I did *exactly* that at your age. I was so excited to follow a new course that I spent a total of ten seconds thinking about the new route before casting off and getting underway. Heck, all I could think about was what the town across the bay was like — I didn't give the new course a second thought. I was daydreaming about the night life in that town right up until my engine died in the middle of the channel."

Tim looked surprised and asked, "Wait, did you say your engine died on your very first trip across the bay?"

Peter leaned back in his chair and put his hands behind his head as a toothy smile appeared on his face. "Yep, I ran out of diesel fuel! How about that one, Tim? I ran out of diesel fuel smack dab in the middle of the day, when ship traffic was at its busiest, and to make matters worse, my boat was much slower than the bigger ships behind me. I almost got run over! I had to turn out of the channel and ended up drifting onto a sandbar. Worse still, because the bay was so busy, the tow fleet couldn't fetch me until the end of the day." Tim looked both shocked and bewildered, which made Peter laugh. Tim didn't under-

Ran out of diesel fuel

stand. How could Peter laugh about running out of diesel fuel, getting stranded on a sandbar, and then having to sit there the rest of the day?

The master and commander laughed loudly while remembering his misfortune, until Tim finally interrupted. "Ah, Peter, am I missing something here? I don't see what's so funny."

Peter took a moment to compose himself, wiping his eyes dry with his sleeve. "Oh, Tim, there was nothing funny about it that day," he said. "I didn't want to show my face on a pier for years!"

"Then why are you laughing? I ran aground yesterday and can't imagine telling anyone about it, let alone laughing about it," Tim said sternly.

Peter regained his composure and leaned forward to let Tim know he understood. "I felt just as you do when it happened to me. I took my failure so personally that I sulked for weeks. I couldn't look another captain in the eye, and my friends made fun of me every chance they got. It was the worst experience of my early career. Now I find it funny, because I know I wouldn't let it happen again. It's not a failure anymore; it's a lesson learned."

The younger captain continued to look skeptical. Peter noticed and continued, "Look, Tim, I've failed many more times than I've succeeded, but I've learned to treat failures not as negatives, but as positives. I use them to understand what doesn't work. To be a master and commander, you must embrace failure as a positive, *not* a negative. When charting your own course, you'll naturally push your own boundaries, and you will figure out things that don't work on your way to understanding what does."

Peter's voice turned deep and raspy as he mimicked his long-ago mentor: "The grand old master and commander that taught me the code would say, 'The only real mistake is the one from which we learn nothing.' "

Tim squirmed in his chair as he imagined that someday he might laugh at running his boat aground. Then, squinting with concentration, he asked his next question: "Okay, so I believe what your master and commander told you, but this goes against everything we learned at Uptoyou University. You don't get ahead by making mistakes on exams, and you certainly don't laugh about them afterward. So I don't get why I should fail in order to learn new things." Peter sat up and took a sip of water, nodding his head patiently. "I didn't say you should fail so you can learn new things. I said, 'When you fail, learn from it.' This is important, because failing is normal; it's part of the learning process, and the sooner you embrace that, the better a captain you'll become. As for what is taught in school, you're right. An exam is not a place to make mistakes; your homework is the place to make mistakes."

Tim looked relieved. He had been starting to wonder whether this sea captain was leading him down a path that would encourage him to throw out everything he had ever learned in school. Peter continued, "But how many of those exams you took at the university did you ace?"

Tim knew that answer. "Ah, not a one," he said.

"I know that feeling," Peter said encouragingly, "but how many times did you go back and try to understand why you missed those questions on all those exams?"

"I ... I didn't do that very often. I was just happy to have the exam behind me," Tim admitted.

"Same here!" Peter exclaimed. "But when you're following your own course, it's like a final exam every day, except you don't have a teacher telling you whether you made a mistake. You have to learn it yourself. And the only way to keep track of what works and what doesn't is to have a plan."

Tim was beginning to grasp the master and commander's message, and Peter could tell. "Tim, I didn't have a plan that day I ran out of fuel, nor on the day I tried to leave the harbor. But now I know how to plan, and that gives me a system for tackling new courses with confidence."

"Okay, I think I'm getting it, but your plan sounds different from the plans they taught us in school. There we learned to plan our day or how to study for a test. What's different about your planning method?"

"Great question!" Peter nearly jumped out of his seat as he pointed his right index finger directly at Tim's chest. "The planning I'm talking about is called '3-D planning.' "

"Huh?" Tim said, bewildered by the term.

"Three-dimensional planning," Peter said. "School is great for learning concepts. They teach you linear, straightforward thinking: To get to C from A, you first go to B. But when you're at sea by yourself, there's nothing linear about it. You need to be thinking three-dimensionally all the time. You have to be aware of the wind, water, waves, and weather, not to mention things such as your engine speed, course, depth, ship speed, and navigation and communication gear."

Tim nodded. He understood these concepts well enough.

"A linear plan won't help when you're at sea," Peter said. "Heck, it didn't help you or me when we tried crossing the bay for the first time! When you plan your own course, Tim, you need to do it three-dimensionally and consider all the things that can go wrong, and then come up with a contingency plan. Some captains call this 'out-of-the-box' thinking, but I prefer to call it 3-D planning. Think of it as looking at a plan from every angle. And guess what?"

"What? I don't know. What?" Tim said with a perplexed look on his face.

"Even with all the planning you do, you'll miss something, and that's when it gets exciting!" Peter exclaimed, looking almost crazed.

"I'm not following you," Tim said. "What's so exciting about a flawed plan?"

Peter jumped to his feet. "Tim, that's the moment when you *learn something new!* That's why it's *exciting!* Do you get it? You use all your knowledge to think three-dimensionally and put together a perfect plan, only to learn you've missed something. But that something will make you smarter and will enable you to do something new. *Now that's exciting!*"

Tim couldn't help but get a little fired up about what the grand master was saying, even though the thought of learning something new at sea scared him. "Ah, I get it!" Tim shouted. "That's why you said to embrace failure as a way to learn. Failure is what makes you smarter; it provides the answers and enables you to become a better captain."

"That's *exactly* right!"

Just then a thought hit Tim, and Peter could see the energy rush out of him almost as quickly as it had entered.

"But Peter, if what you're saying is true, then no plan is perfect, and if that's the case, why bother planning in the first place?"

Peter beamed. Tim was catching on.

"*Excellent question!* So glad you asked!" Peter said encouragingly, to ensure that Tim's questions kept flowing. "You plan to prepare yourself for the unexpected. A grand old master and commander I know has a brass plaque mounted directly above his compass to remind him hourly of these words: 'Luck favors the prepared.'" Peter paused to let Tim transcribe the words onto his notepad, then, tempering his excitement, said slowly, "To prepare, one must first plan. The better your plan, the better you can prepare; the better you prepare, the better your chances of success."

The teacher paused while Tim put pen to paper, then offered one more waypoint to understanding Action #2: "And I've heard other masters and commanders frame the importance of planning in a more negative light." As Tim stopped taking notes and popped his head up, Captain Peter lowered his voice and continued, "What they say is, 'Failure to plan is planning for failure.' " Then the wily skipper sat back in his chair and watched these words sink in.

"So there you have it, Tim—two different ways to emphasize the importance of Action #2: the glass half-empty or the glass half-full approach. I prefer the half-full approach. Fortune favors the prepared."

Peter smiled, knowing that Tim now understood the importance of planning in order to succeed. Tim returned to his notepad and added: *ACTION #2: PLAN IN 3-D* — *think about all angles of the plan, not just where I want to go, but the things that could change my course, and plan how to deal with them.*

The older sea captain was impressed with Tim's willingness to learn and decided to teach him one more action before dinner. Peter picked up a small brass bell on his cocktail table and gave it three short rings, much the way a captain sounds a ship's whistle when backing away from a pier. Within seconds, an older, distinguished gentleman appeared in a crisp, white uniform and spoke with an unusual accent: "Sir, may I be of service?"

Speaking appreciatively, Peter said to the older man, "Jacques, my colleague will join me for dinner this evening." Peter looked at Tim to see if he approved of the dinner invitation. Tim nodded, and Peter added, "Please prepare a dinner of local seafoods, and let's make it fun; surprise us with your selections, Jacques."

The chef bowed slightly and said, "It will be my pleasure, sir. Dinner will be served at 1800 hours." Then he returned to the galley. Peter looked at his chronometer and said, "Perfect. We have thirty minutes to cover the next two actions."

HOW TO GET STARTED

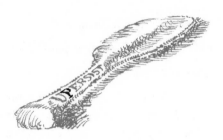

Action #2: Plan in 3-D

"I don't care how many push-ups you can pump out or how many bullets you put in a bull's-eye — if you can't plan a mission, you have no right leading a mission. Failure to plan is a plan for failure, which means your SEAL career will be a short one." The SEAL instructor had our undivided attention. He was leading a pilot program in SEAL team to prepare junior officers for the role of platoon commander. The course was taught by seasoned officers and enlisted leaders from within the SEAL community. There were about ten of us in the class, representing the newest crop of junior officers to report to both the East and West Coast SEAL teams.

Our instructor was one of the more decorated SEAL officers in the community. He had served in most modern SEAL operations from the end of the Vietnam War through Desert Storm One. He was also a rarity within the SEALs; he was a mustang officer, one who had started as an enlisted SEAL, climbed the ranks, and been selected to transfer to the officer ranks. Lieutenant Commander Smith (actual name withheld) brought a powerful perspective to our junior officer training classroom with his firsthand experience as both a follower and a leader.

When he spoke, we listened. Though I've paraphrased his remarks about mission planning, I will never forget their intensity. He could rattle off a list of SEALs who had died because they or their platoon commanders hadn't planned their missions properly. Instructor Smith's intensity had the desired effect; I never forgot what he taught us about how to plan for mission success. Action #2 is based on his teachings. The essentials of SEAL mission planning are no different from those of Milestone Goal planning. Planning is nothing more than preparing, and the more you prepare, the better your chances of success. Every SEAL mission has three phases: Insertion, Actions on the Objective (AOO), and Extraction. Here's how they translate:

- **Insertion:** How will you reach the target?

- **AOO:** What will you do when you reach the target?

- **Extraction:** How will you get home?

This is the basic framework of any mission. Of course, there's much more to planning for mission success than understanding these phases. None of it is hard; it just takes time, creativity, commitment, and perspective. Training for a SEAL mission and going after your own Milestone Goal both require three-dimensional planning. I call Action #2 "Plan in 3-D" not only because great planning requires thinking in three dimensions, but also because each of those dimensions begins with the letter "D." Remember, it's not about creating a perfect plan, because there is no such thing. It's about creating a plan to succeed no matter what obstacles you encounter:

- **Define it:** Define your goal. Be specific. Know the answers to these questions: What are you after *and* when do you want it? If you don't know your goal, you won't know how to measure your progress, and if you can't measure your progress, you won't be able to achieve it. Once you've defined your goal, WRITE IT DOWN and post it in a place where you will see it daily, even hourly. Never allow yourself to forget your mission. Your goal must always be on your mind.

- **Divide it:** Once you know your goal, you can create an action plan. Start by dividing each action into bite-size daily steps you can take to meet your goal. Think of it as smashing your Milestone Goal with a sledgehammer in order to reduce it to small pebbles you collect every day. Rome wasn't built in a day, nor is your Milestone Goal; daily progress is the secret of success.

- **Do it daily:** Feeling like you're making progress is critical to keeping you motivated as you pursue your goal. Get in the habit of asking yourself every morning, "What action can I take today toward my goal?" No two days will be the same, but work toward your goal *every* day. Remember, no matter how small your progress, it's still progress. And to ensure you're learning what works and what doesn't, review your progress daily.

Understand the actions that are helping you make the progress you seek. Daily action is the key to success.

The goal of planning is to create a mindset for success. The planning process conditions your mind for what you need to do to accomplish your goal. It is an important part of turning your dream, your Milestone Goal, into reality. Planning helps you visualize what needs to be done and shows you the sacrifices you must make to achieve your goal. It gets you in the right frame of mind to go after your goal. Remember, however, that a plan is a step in your journey to success; it's *not* the destination. Be aware of "planning paralysis"—getting so wrapped up in creating the perfect plan that you never take any action toward your goal. Your plan is only as good as the actions you take. No plan is perfect. In the SEAL teams, we would say there are two plans: the one you create before a mission, and the one you carry out during the mission. Never forget that the mission is to accomplish your goal, *not* create a pretty plan for it.

Step One: **Define It**

There's nothing complicated about planning. The only challenge is deciding what you want and what you're willing to sacrifice to get it. The trick is to link passion and purpose to your goal. It doesn't matter which comes first, but you need both to keep you inspired. For example, I am passionate about teamwork, adventure, boats, and guns, which made being a SEAL an attractive career for me. However, those passions were not enough during training when I was so cold I vomited or when all my toenails needed to be drilled to relieve the pressure from fluid that had collected in my feet while standing for 72 hours. I needed to find a purpose in becoming a SEAL that would keep me *Fired Up* at the most critical times. I thought long and hard about why I wanted to be a SEAL, and I'm glad I did, because it was my mindset that got me through training. I wasn't the fastest runner or swimmer, nor was I the strongest at doing push-ups or pull-ups, but what I lacked in physical prowess I made up for in determination. I watched my BUD/S (Basic Underwater Demolition/SEAL training) class dwindle from 122 to 18 in the first six weeks of training. The difference between those who made it through the winter Hellweek in December 1991 and those who didn't had nothing to do with bicep size. It had everything to do with how personally important our purpose for being there was to each of us — the survivors wanted it much more than the other 104 men.

No SEAL goes on a mission without knowing its objective. Plain and simple, KNOW YOUR GOAL! Know why you want it and what you're willing to give up to get it. Passion can lead you to a goal worth going after, but purpose keeps you going. Whether your goal is to become a SEAL, start a business, or lose thirty pounds (all past goals of mine), you must define your purpose, get passionate about it, and go after it.

Step Two: **Divide It**

When we started BUD/S Class 181 training, two curious classmates wanted to know the schedule for Hellweek, which was five weeks away. They somehow managed to find a copy. The schedule included many tasks we hadn't been trained to do and allowed us only three-and-a-half hours of sleep for the entire week, which went from Sunday evening to Friday afternoon. The two classmates asked others if they wanted to see the schedule, and most declined, including me. Guess what happened? Those two guys couldn't get that schedule out of their minds. It was so daunting that they began to question themselves and ultimately psyched themselves out long before Hellweek started. They both quit in the second week of training. (I believe the instructors left the Hellweek schedule out on their desks on purpose — they wanted to psyche out anyone they could!)

The point is, one can't get through Hellweek in a day, and you can't accomplish your goal in a day. Folks ask me all the time, "How did you make it through SEAL training?" My first response is always: The only way to make it through training is to focus on the task at hand — the next step, the next breath. (I save my follow-up response for those joining the Navy and attempting SEAL training. That's when I discuss defining their purpose for becoming a SEAL.) And that's the reason behind Step Two — you *must* divide your plan into bite-size goals. For example, if you want to lose thirty pounds, you won't do it in a day or a week or even a month. You'll do it by watching what you eat and working out every day. Losing thirty pounds, starting a business, and completing Hellweek require exactly the same planning approach: divide the objective into daily or even hourly tasks. (During Hellweek I counted seconds!) If you can't complete a small portion of your goal in a day, you've made the goal too big. One day at a time — that's how to accomplish your goal.

Step Three: **Do It Daily**

As I mentioned earlier, no plan is perfect. The only plan that matters is the one you take action on. Through action you'll learn what was originally missing from your plan. If your actions result in failure, embrace it — you just learned something! The only real failure is the one you don't learn from. Thomas Edison used to say, "I learned 10,000 ways not to invent the light bulb." He used failure as a learning tool, and that's exactly the mindset to embrace when going after a Milestone Goal. In the SEALs we'd say, "If you're not failing, you're not trying hard enough." When people ask me how launched Perfect Pushup, I tell them we learned $1,475,000 worth of ways how not to launch a product. (We raised $1.5 million and had $25,000 left when we launched the Perfect Pushup.) However, even though we had nearly run out of money, we still had determination. After the successful launch of Perfect Pushup, it was recognized by *Inc. Magazine* as the fastest-growing consumer-products company in the country in 2009. That was a far cry from two years earlier, when we had been on the brink of bankruptcy.

Whether you're starting a company or reporting for SEAL training, a focus on daily progress will enable you to win the race. Milestone goals are marathons, not sprints. Sometimes you'll feel like you've made no progress or even gone backward. That's okay. It's part of the journey. Remind yourself how far you've come by reviewing your progress and the actions that are helping you. In SEAL team, we call this review, the Debrief. After every mission we have a Debrief of what worked and what didn't. Use the Debrief mindset to help focus on your progress, *not* the distance remaining to your goal. Such negative thoughts are self-destructive. The best way to keep looking forward is to make progress, and the best way to make progress is to work on your goal *every* day. Before you know it, "do it daily" will become a habit, and you'll start asking yourself every morning what you can do to make progress toward your goal. This is a critical step toward being unstoppable and succeeding at anything.

"**A**re you ready, Tim?" Peter asked.

Tim couldn't respond fast enough. He didn't know whether he was more excited about hearing the master and commander's wisdom or eating the remarkable meal he was sure to have this evening.

"Standing by to receive, Cap'n!" Tim said with a smile.

"Good. Then discuss the importance of preparation."

Tim interjected, "The better the plan, the better I can prepare, which makes my chances of success infinitely better."

"Precisely!" exclaimed Peter. "Now, time for a question: Do you know the number-one limiting factor in your ability to properly prepare and execute a plan?"

Tim winced at hearing another question. "My ability to stay focused?" he asked. It was a shot in the dark, but better than he'd done in response to the master and commander's earlier questions.

Action #3
Exercise to Execute

"Actually, that's a close second," Peter said. "Staying focused —
not getting side-tracked — is definitely an important factor in
preparing and executing your plan. But the *number-one* factor in turning your plan into reality is your ability to do work."

Once again, Tim sat across from Peter with a quizzical look on his
face and slowly said, "Ooo-kay, right, got it — my ability to do work.
Is that Action #3?"

"It's part of the third action—the first part," Peter stated, as if
guiding a student through a mathematical word problem. "The third
action has two parts, and the second part can be completed without
the first part, but you won't be nearly as effective if you don't include
the first part."

Now Tim was confused. He had never been good at word problems, let alone riddles. He wished the captain would provide the answer. But the older captain was enjoying making the young skipper
think, and his next question caught Tim totally off guard.

"Do you know how your body works?" Peter asked with a tone of
curiosity.

Tim was thrown so far off course that he responded with another question. "Do you mean, do I know how my ship works?" he said cautiously.

"No, I mean your body—the one that has two arms and two legs, a head, and a heart," Peter said, tilting his head and smiling as he watched Tim writhe in his chair.

"Ah, well, yeah, of course I do...." Tim paused, squinting, then asked, "Is this a trick question, Peter?"

The trim older captain smiled, closed his eyes for an extra second, inhaled, and said, "No it's not a trick question, Tim, but it's an important one. Most people don't understand or appreciate how and why the body works." It was the second time that evening that Peter had made Tim feel uncomfortable. What did going after dreams have to do with the human body? But he quickly composed himself and listened intently to what Peter said next.

"Your body is designed to do one thing and one thing only. Do you know what that is?"

Tim squirmed again and said uncertainly, "To live?"

Peter responded with a soft but encouraging letdown. "Well, you're sort of right, yes, that's the end result, but not exactly the answer I'm looking for."

The young captain grimaced, knowing his teacher wasn't going to spoon-feed him the answer. He looked to the ceiling as if hoping to find the answer overhead. The master and commander could tell Tim was stuck and added a hint. "Tim, what's the only body part that modern science hasn't been able to transplant into another body?"

Peter remained quiet as Tim searched for an answer and softly repeated the question. "What's the only body part... not transplanted into another body? What's the only body part...." He started naming key components of the body: eyes, kidneys, liver, lungs, heart. Then Tim sat bolt upright and blurted out, "Brain! The brain is the only organ that can't be transplanted!"

"Exactly!" Peter beamed, seeing the satisfaction Tim got from answering the question correctly. "And what is your body designed to do with the brain?"

Tim slouched again in defeat and said the first thing that came to mind. "Uh, protect it?"

"Yes!" Peter yelled. Tim sat back in his chair as if blown by a strong gust of wind. "Yes, your body protects your brain and it also...?" Peter tried to elicit the rest of the answer. Tim returned a blank stare. "It also *obeys* your brain," Peter said. "This is an important concept. Every action you take is one you have control over. We'll discuss this in more detail with the fifth action, but understand this fundamental truth: *Your body obeys your brain.*"

Peter was passionate about the relationship between the body and the brain. It frustrated him to see the next generation of captains finishing school with their bodies in such poor shape. He would often remark to Jacques, the *Persistence*'s chef, "No wonder there aren't more captains trying to leave the harbor; they don't have the stamina or the strength to handle the long hours of work required to cross an ocean. And they probably lack the confidence to do the job."

Peter believed that people who feel good about themselves have the confidence to try new things, and that exercise is one of the best ways to feel good about oneself. Now he sought to emphasize his point. "Your body feeds and protects your brain. Every system in your body is designed to support your brain, from your cardiovascular system, which

Posture

pumps it full of oxygenated blood and nutrients, to the neurological system, which gives it the pathways to issue orders to your muscular/skeletal system, which in turn produces motion. And motion means work." Peter let the words drift around the room for a moment and watched Tim's eyes perk up upon recognizing the connection between the body and the brain.

"The reason I'm focusing on this physiological fundamental, Tim, is that most people neglect their body, even though it's our most important asset when it comes to turning our dreams into reality."

Tim nodded slowly, catching Peter's drift.

"Your brain is your command center that decides whether you can or can't do something. It is completely dependent on the input it receives from your body. Feed your body bad foods, and your brain slows down, making it harder to make decisions. The same thing happens when you don't exercise." Peter jumped to his feet to demonstrate poor posture and an extended stomach. "Your body's condition can directly impact your physical stamina, which you will need by the boatload when venturing off on a new course."

Peter paced in front of Tim as he explained the importance of exercise and a healthy diet when pursuing big dreams. "Did you know that exercise combats about fifty different ailments, from diabetes to depression?" he asked. "Exercise and healthy foods are your best medicine. Exercise also helps build stamina, and that is *exactly* what you'll need when you're at sea by yourself for long periods of time. And you know what else you'll need at sea when doubt comes knocking and you're wondering if you're on the right course?" Peter didn't give Tim time to respond. "A positive attitude! You'll need many helpings of positive, can-do spirit. And guess what happens when you exercise?"

The whites of Tim's eyes showed all around his pupils as he watched Peter stomp about.

"*Exercise* fires up the can-do endorphins, the ones that combat depression," Peter said. "Exercise is your single best defense against giving up! Are you tracking with me?"

Now it all made sense to Tim. He had wondered how this older captain had managed to carry his diving equipment so effortlessly on board his ship. And then there was his iron-grip handshake and his youthful energy. Tim could see it in his eyes. This older man was stronger and fitter than he. The young captain was catching on.

Tim smiled. "I'm tracking with you, Peter. I get it!"

Peter took a deep breath. He was living proof that exercise could keep a captain young, inspired, and brimming with can-do, positive energy.

"So, what's exercise got to do with Action #3, you ask?" Peter didn't wait for Tim's response. "Exercise strengthens the body, and the more resilient the body, the more endurance you have. The more endurance you have, the more effectively you can execute your plan. Make sense?" The master and commander directed his laser focus into Tim's eyes. "It's all about executing, and exercise helps. I'm all for anything that helps me execute better or more efficiently. It's all about executing when you're out of the harbor and going after your big hairy dream." The commander sat down in his chair and took a couple of deep breaths.

"So is exercise part one of Action #3?" Tim asked. He wanted to get the action on paper and keep the teacher on course.

"It is. It's the first part of the third action, and if you can't tell by now, I believe it is critical," Peter said with a wink.

"Oh, I get your point loud and clear, Skipper," Tim said, winking back at Peter. "Then what's the other part?"

"The other part is to execute daily," Peter said matter-of-factly. "Tim, going after a dream takes time, stamina, and momentum. Life has so many distractions that it can be easy to drift off-course while following a dream. You need to build a habit of executing your plan D-A-I-L-Y." Peter said the last word slowly and clearly, as if spelling it out loud. "Your plan is only good if you can execute it. Plans are only plans until you turn them into actions, and exercise can help keep you going when you feel like giving up. I consider exercise part of executing a plan. I do it first thing every morning. It stokes my engine all day as I tackle the intricacies of executing my plans."

The young captain let a smile cross his face. He was starting to understand what made Peter such a strong captain. Tim was more and more convinced that he wanted to follow a similar life's journey. He was inspired by the master and commander's energy, strength, and stamina. If exercise provided Peter with those qualities, Tim wanted to exercise too. The more he heard the spry captain speak, the more Tim wanted to be just like him.

"So, what do you call Action #3, Peter?" Tim asked. "I get how exercise helps you execute and I understand that I need to build a daily habit of executing my plan, but how do you define the action?"

"Oh, that's simple," Peter said. "I call it 'Exercise to Execute Daily.'" With pride in his voice, he continued, "Trust me on this one, and promise me that if you decide to follow the code, you won't blow off the exercise portion of this action. I can't tell you how many times it has saved me both mentally and physically. There's no way I could have crossed the great blue ocean without the stamina that exercise gave me to stand watch for countless hours or to work day and night with the Eskimos to weld the steel plates onto my ship's hull so we could beat the ice flows out of the Northwest Passage." Peter shivered as he reflected on that memory. "I can honestly say, Tim, that exercise has saved my ship and my life. When you're stuck, really stuck, and you want to turn around, head for home, and give up for good, take a one-hour break and get your heart pumping. Pick any exercise you enjoy — I like using the rowing machine — and then return to tackle the problem. I promise you will have a new outlook and a clear mind ready to solve your particular problem. It works every time."

The student nodded, then scribbled in his notepad, emphasizing the first word: *Exercise* to execute daily! He retraced the letters of the word "exercise" three times and imagined the exercises he would perform daily. Then a waft of intoxicating smells drifted by Tim's nose, interrupting his train of thought.

The fresh scents had a similar effect on Peter, who broke the silence with a proclamation: "I believe Jacques is preparing one of my favorite meals, pan-seared Ahi tuna." Peter rolled his eyes and tightened his lips, as if already tasting the meal. "Tim, we are in for a rare treat tonight!"

The younger captain was as eager as Peter was to taste the meal, but wanted to keep his mentor talking and providing every possible insight. He desperately wanted time to slow this magical evening down, but knew that time, like the tides, is inevitable. He broke the silence by returning to the topic that had animated the master and commander minutes earlier.

"Peter, this makes so much sense to me. I understand the connection between exercise and my brain. I had never thought of it that way. I also see the link between being in shape and being able to execute a plan. I promise to incorporate exercise into my daily routine. I have one question, though: What do you do when you don't have time to exercise?"

The animated captain laughed. "No one has the time to exercise unless they make it a priority!" he said. Then he stood up, pushed the coffee table aside, dropped to the floor, and started doing push-ups. At the top of his fifth push-up, he turned to Tim and said, "Well, what are you waiting for?"

"You want me to do push-ups ...with you?"

"Absolutely!

Push-ups

The best way to understand something is to experience it. Drop down here and get your blood pumping," Peter commanded with a smirk on his face.

Tim obliged reluctantly, feeling intimidated by the elder captain's vigor and ability to perform push-ups with such ease.

The two men knocked out ten push-ups together, though Tim's face turned red as he struggled to complete his last five. When his arms started to shake, Peter offered encouragement. He could easily have done another thirty push-ups, but stopped at ten so Tim would be motivated, not defeated. Giving the breathless student a congratulatory slap on the back, Peter said, "Now that you know how to do a push-up, you will never need to worry about not having enough time to exercise!" Then Peter returned to relax in his chair.

Tim took a little longer to collect himself, as he hadn't done push-ups since taking a physical education class in high school. He marveled at how easy the older captain made those push-ups look. Then Peter offered some advice.

"I've found push-ups to be the single best exercise when I don't have time for a row or a run. Push-ups engage all the major muscle groups, and you can do them anytime, anywhere. In fact, I use them to help me stay awake when I'm on watch late at night or when I need a mid-afternoon boost after eating too much lunch."

Tim nodded while slowly returning to his note-taking position in the opposite chair. A small bead of sweat dripped down his left temple as he made a mental note to start incorporating push-ups into his daily routine. He took a deep breath, then exhaled slowly and said, "Point taken, Skipper. I have no excuse not to exercise."

"Not to worry, Tim, push-ups have an easy learning curve," Peter said. "Start with sets of three to five repetitions throughout the day, and you'll be knocking them out with ease in a couple of weeks. I make it a game. Sometimes I'll do ten every time I head to the bathroom or get a glass of water. After a long day, when I need to stay awake for a few more hours, I might set an alarm and do ten push-ups every ten minutes. That's a surefire way to stay awake!"

"I'll start with three and see where it takes me," Tim said, still catching his breath.

Peter nodded, looking content, then glanced at the stainless steel chronometer on his wrist and said, "Tim, we have ten minutes until dinner. How about discussing the fourth action until Jacques tells us it's time to sit down at the table?"

"I'm all ears!" Tim said, perking up. Then he pulled the old mahogany coffee table back to its original position so he could return to note-taking and avoid doing any more push-ups.

HOW TO GET STARTED

Action #3: Exercise to Execute

What if I told you of a pill that makes you smarter, helps you lose weight *and* build muscle, fights off depression, improves your ability to work longer and harder, and prevents numerous life-threatening conditions including heart disease and diabetes? What would you pay for this pill—$10, $50, maybe $100?

Now, what if I told you this pill could change your destiny by making you successful and perhaps famous, if fame is a dream of yours? And what if I told you this pill could give you the confidence to do anything you put your mind to? How much might the pill be worth to you now? $1,000? Maybe $10,000?

I'll make it even more interesting: What if I told you this pill comes with zero percent financing? How much debt would you be willing to incur to get the power of this pill?

But wait — there's more! Did I mention that this pill could also help you attract the woman or man of your dreams? Before you decide how much you'd pay for it, take a few minutes to daydream about the power of this pill. Close your eyes and visualize what you would do with this power. Ask yourself: Where would I go? What would I do? Who is the woman or man of my dreams and what would we do together? What would this happiness feel like? Would I change the world? What would I buy with my newfound wealth?

Now that you've considered how good this pill could make you feel, and how it could change the course of your life, what would you think if I told you that you must reserve thirty minutes a day for the pill to work?

Thirty minutes; that's it. Does knowing about this thirty-minute commitment change your mind about how much the pill is worth? I bet it doesn't. I bet you'd give up more than thirty minutes for the power of this pill. Think about the things you do each day that take thirty minutes or more: getting ready for school or work, watching TV, surfing the Internet, reading the newspaper.

Okay, so here's the final catch: The pill doesn't work overnight. You have to take it every day for about thirty days to *feel* a difference, sixty days to *see* a difference, and ninety days to *make* a difference. Still interested in taking the pill? How much does it cost? It's FREE! And there's no time limit on the offer.

The title of Action #3 probably gave you a big clue to the kind of pill I'm referring to, but the beauty of this metaphor is that it's 100 percent true. Okay, so exercise doesn't come in a pill, and you have to work during the thirty minutes mentioned above, but exercise can be your secret weapon for making your dreams come true. I'm living proof. Exercise helped me beat asthma, and it gave me the confidence to try out for my high-school rowing team. My success in rowing led to being recruited to the Naval Academy, where I gained the courage to try out for the SEALs. As a SEAL, I became a student of exercise and learned how to use it to unlock my potential. Exercise led me from the SEALs to business school to inventing the Perfect Pushup. Exercise has been my swim buddy throughout my life. It's given me the confidence and courage to face my fears, the stamina and strength to go after my dreams, and yes, I even credit exercise with helping me attract the woman of my dreams.

I know I've oversimplified my Milestone Goals and highlighted exercise as the key driver in achieving them. I'm not saying exercise was the only thing that helped me beat asthma, win rowing championships, graduate from SEAL training, invent successful products, and find the love of my life. What I *am* saying is that my successes started with exercise. It has been my catalyst for dreaming up new ideas, it gets me *Fired Up* to go after them, and it gives me the endurance to forge ahead when others call it quits. Exercise keeps my brain focused and my attitude positive — it powers my call to action. When I get stuck, I take a break and pop a thirty-minute exercise pill. Exercise clears my mind and helps me get unstuck. In SEAL training, instructors would offer a simple solution when doubt cluttered our minds: "When in doubt — push 'em out!" As much as we despised doing tens of thousands of push-ups during training and our careers in the teams, they remain one of the simplest and most effective forms of exercise. I use them to wake up in the morning, stay awake during long stretches of intense work, or celebrate an occasion. (I know the last reason sounds weird, but there's no better way to ramp up your enthusiasm for something than using the endorphins you get from knocking out twenty push-ups!) There's a reason instructors use push-ups as a staple exercise throughout all four phases of SEAL training; push-ups work every major muscle group of your body. Think about it: To do a push-up you must perform a deep squat (leg muscles), extend both legs out (core and back muscles), get into the starting plank position (core, back, arm, and shoulder muscles), and then lower yourself to the ground and push back up again (chest, arms, and abs). Do this repeatedly and your heart gets pumping — really pumping — as if you were sprinting (cardio). The longest stretch I ever spent on a submarine was fifty-five days; can you guess what exercise kept me sane in those confines? Push-ups! My teammates and I would play push-up games with a deck of cards by naming each suit a different form of a push-up and then seeing how many times we could repeat the deck before utter exhaustion set in. The last man pushing 'em out won. The beauty of the push-up is that you can do it anywhere and anytime. If Jack Palance can knock out push-ups while receiving an Academy Award, then we can also do them anywhere and anytime! I've been known to drop down in the middle of a meeting and knock out ten push-ups to honor someone's accomplishment. People find humor in it and I get a charge from it — it's a win-win. There are very few excuses that can prevent you from knocking out push-ups throughout the day. I've even watched double-leg-amputee veterans knock out push-ups. If they can do it, so can the rest of us! Push-ups help you burn fat, build muscle, and boost your brain power — that's right, brain power. The chemical reaction that occurs when you challenge your muscles and force your heart to work harder by pumping blood from your legs to your arms and back again (squatting, pushing, and standing up) triggers the release of powerful hormones called endorphins. These hormones act like a natural drug for the body by calming and focusing the brain. They produce dopamine, often called the happy hormone, which powers a positive attitude and helps fight depression. Endorphins can help us sleep better, improve our sex drive, and stimulate blood flow to improve circulation, which enhances brain function, enabling us to better process information and making us smarter. How many more reasons do you need to start doing push-ups now that you know they will positively change your life? The power of exercise is so overwhelmingly convincing and so thoroughly documented that I seriously contemplated focusing this entire book on how to inspire folks to use exercise to their advantage. But life isn't as simple as just doing push-ups. To reach a Milestone Goal you must perform thousands of hours of actions. Going after life-changing goals takes both commitment and hard work — lots of it. In his book *The Tipping Point,* Malcolm Gladwell states that you need to perform 10,000 hours of work to master a skill. That's equivalent to five years if you put in an honest forty-hour work week for fifty weeks a year (everyone needs a vacation; two weeks off is a good thing). To do this with sustained vigor and unrelenting determination, you need stamina, and where do you think this stamina will come from? Coffee? Energy drinks? NO! These are short-term boosts that can have long-term negative consequences. The sugar in energy drinks can lead to weight gain, even diabetes. These drinks may make you feel full of energy at first, but you can't avoid the subsequent crash. The same goes for coffee; too much caffeine is bad for the body. Common side effects include headaches, shakes, heart palpations, and drowsiness. I enjoy coffee, but it's no substitute for the energy I naturally produce from exercising. To exercise is to execute. When the SEAL instructors shouted out "When in doubt — push 'em out!" we would get to work. When you get stuck, when you're not sure what to do next, go exercise. It will not only recharge you; it will also give you a sense of accomplishment. This sense of accomplishment can help you think positively when you feel as if you can't go on. The obstacles of your mind will be the most challenging ones you will face in conquering your goals. Doctor Seuss said it best in *Oh, the Places You'll Go!:* "The toughest games you'll play are the games against yourself." These games can only be won with a can-do attitude. You will question yourself; that's normal. Humans are wired to avoid pain and pursue pleasure. Work is painful by its nature, but we persevere for its rewards. The best way to win these mind games is to create a daily habit of working toward your goal. You will need strength, stamina, and energy to keep going, and there's only one way to get those things: exercise.

Not sure how to get started? No problem. Try the plan below. It's an exercise-habit-forming, twenty-one-day plan to help you work toward your goal. I find that the best time to exercise is first thing in the morning; it's too easy to tell yourself that you'll do it later in the day and then find excuses not to. Don't make any excuses; just do it!

Day 1: How many push-ups can you do without stopping? Be honest and stop as soon as you can no longer perform a push-up using perfect form. Can't do a push-up from the plank position? No problem; drop your knees to the floor and do as many as possible from that starting position.

Day 2: Go for a thirty-minute walk. Can't do thirty straight minutes? No problem; divide it into shorter times until you can do it! If you can only do five minutes at a time, do that six times for a total of thirty minutes over the course of the day.

Day 3: Perform your maximum number of push-ups one at a time. For example, if you can do ten, start in the standing position, squat down, perform a push-up, stand back up, and repeat nine more times.

Day 4: Repeat Day 2.

Day 5: Repeat Day 3.

Day 6: Repeat Day 2.

Day 7: Have fun and go outside to play!

Day 8: Perform a one-set maximum of push-ups again, but afterward stand up and do as many individual ones (standing between each one) as possible. How many extra ones can you do: three, five, seven, more? Whatever the number, make it your new maximum.

Day 9: Go for a thirty-minute walk. Even if you had to use six increments of five minutes each in Day 2, you can probably do it all at once now.

Day 10: Do your new maximum number of push-ups one at a time, standing between each one.

Day 11: Repeat Day 9.

Day 12: Repeat Day 10.

Day 13: Repeat Day 9.

Day 14: Repeat Day 10.

Day 15: Go have fun!

Day 16: Perform a one-set maximum of push-ups, but stand up afterward and do as many individual ones (standing between each one) as possible. How many extra ones can you do: three, five, seven, more? Whatever the number, make it your new maximum.

Day 17: Go for a thirty-minute walk. You're probably covering more distance in thirty minutes now than you were in Day 2 or even Day 9.

Day 18: Do your new maximum number of push-ups one at a time, standing between each one.

Day 19: Repeat Day 17.

Day 20: Repeat Day 18.

Day 21: Repeat Day 17.

Day 22: Get *Fired Up*! You're on your way to being unstoppable!

The master and commander smiled, anticipating the question he planned to ask next. Sitting motionless, he watched the young, out-of-breath captain regain his composure after completing his ten push-ups. Peter remembered what it had been like to be a young captain like Tim, exuberant and eager to learn. Though they hadn't yet discussed all the actions of the code, Captain Peter believed Tim had what it takes to follow the code and become a master and commander. Tim fidgeted as the silence stretched on, fearing that another soul-searching question was coming. And he was right.

Peter leaned forward, resting his elbows on his thighs. "Tim, do you believe in yourself?" he asked.

The question hit Tim like a tidal wave, rushing over and stranding him, just as an equally difficult question had done the day before. He looked left, then right, as if seeking the nearest exit, and rubbed his

Action #4
Recognize Your Reason to Believe

sweaty palms up and down his pant legs, searching for the right response — any response."Ah, what do you mean by that? Like do I believe I'm 'Tim'?" he asked, feigning a half-smile and making fun of the salty captain's question.

"No, I am quite confident you know your name," Peter said, staring into Tim's darting eyes. "I want to know whether you have confidence in yourself." The master waited more than a minute for Tim's response.

"I, I think I do.... Ah, sure, of course I believe in myself..." Tim sputtered. Then puffing out his cheeks like a blowfish and exhaling deeply, he confessed in a soft voice, "I'm not sure." Tim dropped his head, as he avoided Peter's gaze.

Not wanting Tim to wallow a second longer, Peter jumped up and clapped his hands to redirect Tim's attention. "Of course you're not sure! You just ran your ship aground yesterday. And guess what? I've done the same thing. I know *exactly* how you feel. Heck, sandbars are nothing compared to rocks!" With that confession, Peter walked over to a display case directly behind his lounge chair. Standing full height from floor to overhead, the case was bolted in place by a series of stainless steel, L-shaped brackets and housed four glass-paned shelves designed to hold medical supplies. Peter opened the chest-high door and pulled out a large, flat rock. "And speak-

The Kanji stone

ing of rocks," he said, "take a look at this one."

The oblong stone that the master and commander placed in front of the young captain was blue-gray and perfectly smooth on one side. Tim noticed it had something carved into it. "What is this?" he asked, running his fingers over the markings on the stone.

"Those are Japanese words called *Kanji*," Peter said. "This stone was given to me by a Japanese master and commander."

"What does it say?" Tim asked, still admiring the smooth stone.

"Ah, great question. It says, 'Before you can achieve, you must first believe.' It's an important message, and I keep this stone on the third shelf of the display case so that I will see it every time I walk into the wardroom. I never want to forget this message."

Tim nodded while repeating the passage quietly to himself and reaching for his notepad so that he could write the words down.

Peter continued, "The Japanese master likened one's power to believe to a river that will conquer any obstacle in its path. It can flow over some obstacles and go around others by gradually carving its own path. This stone is an example of such an obstacle; it came from the famous Fuji River that flows from Mount Fuji to the sea. The river followed its own course, and even the hardest stone couldn't stop it. It was the *relentless* flow of the river that made the stone smooth."

The hardened skipper lowered his voice and focused on the younger captain as he emphasized the word "relentless." After pausing for a moment to allow the emphasis to sink in, he continued. "The power of a river isn't created in an instant; it builds as it continues to flow. This makes a river unstoppable, and your ability to believe in yourself must do the same thing over time. It must keep flowing — and you must always believe in yourself. Like the river, as you continue to believe in yourself, you will be able to conquer all obstacles in your path."

The young captain nodded, squinting with one eye as if the sound of the last statement had been painful. "So, all I have to do is believe and I can achieve anything I want?" he asked.

"Ha! Tim, if it were only that simple!" Peter responded. "First, you need to *recognize a reason to believe*. And that will come from the small successes in your life. These successes will compound and build your confidence, making you feel empowered to try bigger and bolder tasks. For instance, do you feel ready to steam across the ocean with me tomorrow morning?"

Tim shifted nervously in his chair, he didn't have to say anything for Peter to understand his answer.

"Exactly. Of course not," Peter said. "You're not ready to make that kind of voyage...yet. But you are ready to navigate back across the bay to the south end of Hardwork Harbor."

Tim wasn't so sure; he had butterflies in his stomach just thinking about it. Peter sensed his apprehension and said, "Tim, you must and you will cross that bay. Think about it: You know more about that course than you did before you tried taking it — you now know where that sandbar is!"

Tim perked up. The captain was right. Tim had spent so much time focusing on how embarrassing it was to be towed that he had lost sight of the lesson he had learned: There was a sandbar between buoys 15 and 17.

"Look, you want to know the most important reason I exercise, Tim?" Peter looked at him encouragingly. "I exercise because not only does it give me stamina and strength, it also gives me reason to believe in myself."

The student tilted his head to one side, looking perplexed. "Huh?" he mumbled.

"Yep, that's right," Peter said. "Exercise gives me the confidence that I can conquer whatever is in my control. When I was your age and learning the code, I was about twenty-five pounds overweight. The first thing my master and commander taught me was to take control of my body. 'Take control of your body and you'll take control of your life,' he said." Peter paused for a moment to allow Tim to finish taking notes. "I didn't have anything to lose except weight, so I decided to start exercising. At first, I felt only a small rush of adrenalin and some extra energy from the exercise, but as my body started to change, I could feel my confidence building. I was changing my body and that made me feel successful; it empowered and emboldened me to succeed at other things. By the time I reached my goal of losing twenty-five pounds, I was no longer thinking about weight loss. Instead I was thinking about how I could apply my new-found power — my belief in myself — to bigger and bolder ideas, such as crossing an ocean."

The young captain sat and stared at his teacher, not knowing what to say. Peter noticed Tim's incredulous look and continued, "Look, whether you're trying to lose twenty-five pounds or travel twenty-five hundred miles across an ocean, you must start by believing you can do it. You don't lose twenty-five pounds in a day, nor can your ship go twenty-five hundred miles in a day. This stone wasn't carved in a day either." The master ran his hand over the stone, simulating the flow of a river. "But through *relentless* action, you too will cross that ocean. And to sustain *relentless* action you must believe in yourself and the goal you seek to accomplish. Do you copy what I'm transmitting, Skipper?" Peter didn't wait for Tim to answer. "The more you believe in yourself, the harder you'll try and, when that happens, you'll learn there's nothing you can't do. The trick is separating the beliefs that help you from those that hinder you."

Tim twisted suddenly as if he were dodging a punch and asked, "Hold on, Captain, I was with you on recognizing my reason to believe in order to succeed, but what do you mean by beliefs that hinder me?"

"Throughout our lives we develop our own beliefs in order to survive and thrive, but some of those beliefs can conflict with our future courses. When that happens, they can hinder our progress. Sometimes these long-held beliefs can prevent us from ever trying a new course." Peter leaned forward and used his hands to further emphasize the point. "Tim, what we believe dictates our actions, which are a direct result of our beliefs. If you believe you can't cross the bay tomorrow, guess what? You won't take the action to cross the bay tomorrow."

Peter paused, though not long enough to let the young captain think about the inevitability of what he had to do the next day. "But the good news is, you've already crossed the bay and know you can do it, and you *will* cross it again," Peter said with a playful smile. "Over time, your belief that led you to take the action of crossing the bay could grow into your reason to believe that you can cross any ocean.

The key is to recognize and focus on the beliefs that will help you accomplish the course you've chosen. It's easier said than done...." The salty skipper paused to reflect on a painful memory of running his boat up on the rocks. "There have been many times throughout my life that I believed I couldn't do something, and you know what?"

"What?" Tim said meekly, as if it were a trick question.

"Every time I believed I couldn't do something, I was right. But only because I hadn't taken action!" Peter became more animated as he moved to the edge of his chair, his stare intensifying and the pitch of his voice rising with excitement. "But here's the beautiful thing: The opposite is also true. Every time I believed I *could* do something, I made progress in the direction of my course. Sometimes it didn't feel like progress, as I only learned a few ways *not* to do something, but it was still progress because I didn't give up believing I could do it! Get it?" Peter paused just long enough for his pupil to nod. Then he lowered his voice, narrowed his gaze, and said, "Tim, remember what I told you earlier: 'Whether you believe you can or you can't, you're right.' "

Tim's lips moved quietly as he recited the master and commander's words. Then he nodded his head slowly as a smile started spreading from the right edge of his mouth. "I...I think I'm tracking with you," he said. "So what you're saying is that my beliefs power my actions or my inactions, depending on what I believe I can or can't do — and what I can or can't do is totally up to what I *believe* I can or can't do, right?"

"Dead-on, Captain!" Peter shouted as he jumped to his feet and clapped his hands in one thunderous motion. "You couldn't be more correct, Tim! What you believe decides what you *can* or *can't* do!"

The eager student leaned back in his chair, relieved and enlightened. And the master and commander sensed it; this was the perfect time to deliver the next park of his message. Placing his hands slowly on the river rock, Peter lowered his head so he was eye level with Tim and said, "The code is all about instilling habits that help you succeed at the things you can control. You can't control the wind, water, or waves, but you can control how you will handle them. You can control the course you take and most importantly, you *can* control your actions and your ability to believe. Once you truly understand this, you *will* succeed at anything you decide to focus on and then, my friend, the oceans and all their abundance will be your oysters — they are just waiting for you to harvest them. The oceans will challenge you, frustrate you, but will make you a better, more knowledgeable captain. Trust me: If you follow the code and never stop believing in yourself and your courses, you *will become unstoppable* at living your dreams."

A broad smile crossed Tim's face. No one had ever spoken to him so positively, so encouragingly. He felt his heart rate climb by a few beats and sensed goose bumps along his forearms and at the nape of his neck. The commander's message made sense. It was so powerful yet simple: Start with small successes, build a reason to believe, and never stop believing. This will make anything possible.

Jacques had been waiting patiently behind the ruby-red curtain at the main galley entrance for the master and commander to finish his speech to the young skipper. The old chef had heard his captain deliver these words on only a handful of occasions, and knew how passionate he was about encouraging the next generation to pursue their own courses. Though the food sat for five extra minutes on the table, the chef was certain the commander wouldn't mind, and Jacques always enjoyed hearing the code repeated; he had used it to follow his own course to becoming a chef.

As the teacher leaned back to watch his student absorb the latest lesson, Jacques cleared his throat and chimed a small brass ship's bell that hung just to the right of the commander's war chest. "Gentlemen, dinner is served," he said. "Please lay to mess for the evening meal." The words hung in the air as both captains stopped to admire each other. The younger captain had a new appreciation for his lessons and his new friend; the older captain admired his pupil for having the courage and desire to follow his own course. Still, the aging master and commander may have gained more during the evening than his apprentice had, as one of his greatest joys was helping others go after their own courses.

The master and commander moved first. "Okay, Tim, let's not keep Jacques' masterpieces waiting. Trust me, you don't want to upset the chef or your palate for that matter; you're in for a real treat!"

Peter clapped his hands and headed toward the feast, motioning for Tim to bring the river rock to the table. Then he asked Jacques what he'd prepared.

"Sir, the menu for the evening meal starts with a local short-spined purple sea urchin surrounded by slices of albacore tuna belly gently brushed with Meyer lemon, ginger, and fresh soy sauce," Jacques said proudly as he stepped away from his creation, which looked more like an exotic flower than food.

Tim nearly dropped the stone when he saw the precise arrangement of the meal on the table. While the round table could seat up to six people, only two chairs were present, and both faced toward the bow of the *Persistence*, one in the 4 o'clock position and the other in the 8 o'clock position. The master and commander took the latter position. An unusual cloth divided the table in half from the 3 to the 9 o'clock position. Hand woven with interlocking, diamond-shaped designs, the cloth was red and blue with contrasting black and white patterns. Three candles cradled in opposing small tusks sat on the remarkable piece of fabric. The bone candelabra flanked a large wooden bowl that nearly overflowed with a variety of fruits, some of which Tim didn't recognize. He was still studying the table when Peter said with a hint of playful authority, "Time, tide, and Jacques' meals wait for no one. Let's eat, Skipper!"

Tim responded in kind: "Aye, aye, Captain!"

The inexperienced captain tried to prepare his taste buds for what he was about to eat, but his brain couldn't process the flavors of the exotic foods. He had never seen such a divine spectacle on a plate. While Tim was deciding what to eat first, Peter chimed in.

"May I suggest you alternate bites between the sea urchin and the tuna? The urchin is salty, and the tuna is like sweet butter," Peter said while lifting a small, iridescent spoon carved from the shell of an abalone and gingerly scooping out a bit of urchin meat from the belly of the spiny delicacy. Tim followed suit and was amazed at the flavors and how harmoniously they blended in his mouth. A couple of bites into the meal, Captain Peter broke the silence by complimenting Jacques on the appetizer: "Bravo, Jacques. You've outdone yourself again. Outstanding!" Jacques peered around the corner from the galley where he was preparing the main course. Nodding and smiling, he said, "Why, thank you, Captain. The next course will be served in eight minutes, sir." Jacques' attention to detail hadn't gone unnoticed by Tim; from his exact timing to the precision with which he prepared the first course, Jacques was a perfectionist. Captain Peter also appreciated the ease with which Jacques carried out a skill that the captain hadn't mastered himself.

As they savored the appetizer, Peter looked at the "believe to achieve stone" that Tim had placed between the two of them on the table, and returned to teaching mode.

"So let's recap before Jacques interrupts us with another distracting creation," Peter said with a wink, just loud enough for Jacques to hear.

"I'll do my best, Cap'n," the chef said. "Seven minutes and counting, sir."

Peter smiled at Tim. "I call Action #4 'Recognize Your Reason to Believe.' Remember this stone; remember the power of a river and how it succeeds. It doesn't do it all at once; this stone was carved by the never-ending flow, the relentless action of the river. To achieve, you must believe, and believing comes from succeeding, and succeeding starts with small successes. Small successes grow to become bigger successes. The more you succeed, the more you will believe in yourself, and the more you believe, the more you'll be *unstoppable.*" Peter's voice sank an octave as he said the word "unstoppable," as if it were rising from his soul. It startled Tim.

"And when you're *unstoppable*, nothing can prevent you from following your course, from achieving your dreams," Peter said. "You'll never give up. When you learn how to maintain your course and speed no matter what comes your way, you will be your own master and commander."

Tim dropped his tuna spoon into the belly of the urchin he had just devoured and began furiously scribbling on his notepad. "I'm reading you loud and clear," he said. "I get Action #4! Believing leads to achieving because it keeps you going when others give up. It's like confidence fuel to power you through rough waters when the course gets tough."

Peter beamed and exclaimed, "Exactly, Tim!"

"This is starting to make sense to me," Tim said. "Actions one, two, and three are designed to create a habit of believing in yourself, to build up your confidence so you don't quit. The code is actually all about..." Tim's voice trailed off as another gear in his brain clicked. Now it made perfect sense. The name of Peter's ship, *Persistence*.... The captain had named his ship after the essence of the code!

"*Persistence!*" Tim shouted, as if conducting a man-overboard drill. Peter smiled from ear to ear as he leaned back in his chair to enjoy Tim's moment of reckoning.

"You named your ship after the meaning of the code," Tim said. "You must see that word a thousand times a day. You did it so you'll never forget what it's all about, didn't you?" Tim didn't wait for an answer as another clue fell into place. "Just like this stone; you placed it where you can see it several times a day to constantly remind yourself of the code!"

Peter smiled and nodded. "I was so excited when I learned the code that I promised myself I would never forget what it stood for, and what better way to never forget than to name your ship after it? So, my ship became the *Persistence*.

"That's a serious commitment to the code, to name your ship after."

"True. But, as you will soon learn, success comes from building habits that enable you to take the correct actions toward fulfilling your dream. I wanted to build a habit that would force me to always remember what the code was about. Sure, I knew I could write the word down in my notebook and consciously remember it from time to time, but I didn't want that; I wanted it out there for the entire world to see. I wasn't the best student in school, nor the best athlete; heck I wasn't even the best ship driver. But I made it my goal to be the best at never giving up — at dreaming big and being personally accountable for making my dreams come true. Naming the ship *Persistence* was another small way to build a habit of remembering daily — even hourly — what it takes to succeed on the course I choose."

The young captain was awed by Peter's passion for not giving up, and equally impressed with his humility. He had been an ordinary student and young captain who had worked extraordinarily hard at pursuing his own dreams. The more Tim heard Peter talk, the more he wanted a life like his.

"Tim, I hadn't planned to show you this yet, but since you put two actions plus two actions together regarding the code, I think it's appropriate." Peter motioned for Tim to join him and called to Jacques for an update on the next dish. Peter had three-and-a-half minutes to show Tim a special plaque attached to the base of the ship's compass.

The wardroom had a mahogany-paneled door hidden to the left of a vintage oil painting of a ship steaming into daunting seas and dark clouds. A ray of light from above burned through the clouds as if to guide the ship through the storm. Peter pressed the panel and the door gave a hiss as fresh sea air wafted by and they entered the bridge of the *Persistence* directly behind the helm. Peter flipped on the red navigation lights and pointed to a plaque below the directional read-out of the compass.

"Go ahead, Tim. Read it out loud." Together, they recited the words: *"Nothing in the world can take the place of persistence. Talent will not; nothing is more common than unsuccessful men with talent. Genius will not; unrewarded genius is almost a proverb. Education will not; the world is full of educated derelicts. Persistence and determination alone are omnipotent. The slogan 'Press On' has solved and always will solve the problems of the human race."*

Tim stood tall and turned, extending his hand to the captain of the *Persistence,* and said, "Thank you, Peter, thank you for showing me the way."

"The pleasure and the honor are all mine," Peter said, giving his apprentice a firm handshake. "Now, let's not upset Jacques; we might just make it back before he's out of the galley."

Returning to the table, Tim tried desperately to remember the exact words on the plaque but couldn't. So Peter repeated them, and just as he finished saying the last word, Jacques appeared.

"Gentlemen, tonight's main course is pan-seared Ahi tuna seasoned with cayenne pepper, olive oil and kosher salt," the chef said. "The steaks are accompanied by a chilled seaweed salad and Yukon gold potatoes lightly dusted with Parmesan truffle oil. Should you need anything, please don't hesitate to call out. Enjoy, gentlemen." And with that, Jacques did a 180-degree about-face and exited the wardroom with appetizer plates in hand. Neither captain spoke as they closed their eyes to let their senses absorb the glorious smells of the remarkable dish in front of them. Tim was still processing what his nose was detecting when Peter said, "Well, no time like the present; let's eat!"

HOW TO GET STARTED

Action #4: Recognize Your Reason to Believe

The first team sport I ever played was basketball at the local YMCA. Our teams were named after NBA teams, and our uniforms resembled those worn by the pros, which in the 1970s meant tank tops and shorts — really short shorts. The tops were tight, the socks came up to our knee caps, and the shorts showed most of our thighs. Most of the eight-year-olds didn't have a problem with the uniforms, but I did. My thighs were huge, while the other players' legs were skinny. As soon as I put those YMCA shorts on, the nicknames started flowing: "Tree Trunks," "Log Legs," and, the one that stuck, "Thunder Thighs." Being a poor basketball player didn't help, nor did my inability to jump more than a couple of inches off the floor. The nickname followed me from the YMCA basketball court to the elementary school playground, where tag was the sport of choice. There I learned I wasn't particularly good at something else: running fast. Over time, I came to accept the nickname, since there wasn't much I could do about the size of my thighs. My mom said that those who made fun of my thighs were really just jealous of my "big powerful legs." I didn't always buy what my mom told me, however; those teammates didn't seem jealous of my legs — they found them funny.

Through eighth grade, I did my best to ignore the nickname Thunder Thighs. That was hard at times, as I wasn't particularly good at traditional sports such as football, soccer, basketball, and baseball. This made me an easy target for getting picked on. As I moved on to high school, how-ever, my athletic situation changed. My new school had a sport that didn't require me to pitch, dribble, or catch, and it was done on water: rowing. I'll never forget my first day of club rowing. Our coach, Professor Johnson, picked me out of the lineup of freshmen and said, "Mills, you've got the legs of an oarsman, big and strong."

That statement changed my view of my thunder thighs. Now they were something to be proud of, not embarrassed about, and they be-came my reason to believe in myself when I tried out for the varsity row-ing team a year later. I didn't have the same rowing experience or upper body strength or lung capacity as the others on the team, but I *knew* I had the thighs to be an oarsman!

At the start of my sophomore year, I teamed up with a senior who was willing to train with me. I dropped all my other sport commitments and focused for the next seven months on training for rowing tryouts. I spent every waking moment thinking about how to earn a seat on one of the two Kent School Boat Club (KSBC) boats. Though I didn't realize it, the club's history of rowing success was legendary, as was W. Hart Perry Jr., the coach who led the crews. His crews had won more championships than any other high school program. Students from around the world came to Kent to pull for Coach Perry. Competition was stiff to earn one of the sixteen seats on each of the two eight-man boats. The first, or var-sity, boat had six returning rowers from the year before, and the second boat had eight returning rowers. That left only two viable seats open, and one of the new sophomores was the younger brother of a first-boat rower and already had rowing experience. He was a lock for a seat, which left one open spot. Had I made a list of all the reasons I should and shouldn't earn that remaining spot on the team, it would have been lop-sided. For starters, my "why I can't make KSBC" list would have included things such as "I have the least amount of rowing experience of everyone trying out"; "I can't do that many pull-ups" (a key exercise for the tryouts); and "I have asthma." On the flip side, my list for "why I can make KSBC" would have had only one bullet point: "I believe I can make it because I was born with rower's legs."

There comes a time during all of life's challenging situations when you have to dig deep inside to find the resolve to keep going. That moment came for me on the last day of rowing tryouts on a bay in Tampa, Florida. I was rowing in the bow of an eight-man boat, and we were racing against another KSBC tryout boat. If we won our race, the seat would be mine; if we lost, I would go home. I had struggled with the two-a-day practices in Florida. Even worse, my hands weren't used to the hours of pulling on a wooden handle, and I had blisters on all my fingers that had popped and turned into open, infected sores. I had to tape my hands into rounded claws and slide the wooden oar handle through the remaining open circle.

Midway through the race, a wave broke over the bow and my back, dousing my hands with salt water. It burned as it worked its way under the tape, and tears rolled down my cheeks as I tried to cope with the pain. The harder I pulled, the more my hands hurt. This was my defining moment, the one when I recognized my reason to believe. As painful as the salt water on my hands felt, the pain of not getting the seat on the boat would be greater. Each day of training had put me in this position, this last race for my seat. I believed I could earn that seat; it didn't matter how much my hands hurt or how unfair it was that my boat hit a wave or that my lungs burned.

We won the race and I earned my seat that day. My life had changed forever. I had learned to believe in myself. As simplistic as it might sound, my big thighs had helped me recognize my reason to believe in making the rowing team. The origin of your reason to believe doesn't matter; what matters is that you recognize your reason to believe in whatever you're going after. Your reason to believe in yourself is your secret weapon for success no matter how big the odds are against you. I can still remember classmates laughing at me for even suggesting that I try out as a sophomore for the KSBC. All the odds were against me, except one, the only one that mattered: my reason to believe. As our great Coach Perry would tell us in preparation for our races, "A crew must first believe, before they can achieve."

Of course, he made sure that our crew's reason to believe didn't rest on my thighs. At the Naval Academy, Coach Clothier, another legendary rowing coach, would have his crews row 2,000 miles a year — a mile for every meter on a standard 2,000-meter race course. His logic was simple: He wanted us to be in better shape than any other crew we raced against. He knew that no other crew would log that many miles. He wanted us to be confident that we had trained harder than any of our competitors. Our reason to believe in ourselves was that we had rowed more miles than the other crews. Your reason to believe can come from anything, but without a reason, you won't accomplish much of anything.

In SEAL training, my reason to believe came from lots of different things. Since the training involved so many challenges, I looked for a reason to believe in everything I did. When it came to diving tests, my reason to believe came from getting my scuba certification with my dad at the age of twelve; when it came to shooting, my reason to believe came from winning rifle competitions at summer camp; when it came to rope climbs and pull-up competitions, my reason to believe came from rowing; when it came to surf torture (enduring cold water), my reason to believe came from winter rowing on the Severn River at the Naval Academy; when it came to running long distances, my reason to believe came from rowing — in fact, most of my reasons for believing in my ability to make it through SEAL training came from rowing. I knew I wouldn't be the fastest runner or swimmer or the strongest at doing push-ups or pull-ups, but I knew I could endure more than most. I would give myself pep talks when bringing up the rear of the platoon in a run or swim. The pep talk was always the same: "Just keep going — take it one step [or one stroke] at a time. I can do one more...." One more stride or swim stroke would turn into another one and then another and another until I got to the finish line. I became the master of taking something one step at a time. No matter what the instructors threw at me, I would find comfort in my reason to believe that I could handle it, because I believed in my ability to keep going. I would do exactly what I did with rowing — one stroke at a time — keep going and keep pulling.

SEALs recognize the importance of believing in yourself and your teammates. That's why all officers and enlisted men go through the same training. Though it's only an initial reason to believe, the training philosophy gives enlisted SEALs a reason to believe in their officers (officers need to earn the respect of their teammates through consistent and sound decision-making and leadership). It's also why Hellweek is so challenging. After going through a week of training that simulates combat, graduates have a reason to believe when they face actual combat. Finding your reason to believe is a critical component in accomplishing your goal. In order to achieve anything, you must first believe you can achieve it.

The key to recognizing your reason to believe is to focus on something you know is true. In ninth grade, I was absolutely certain I had big legs. Then a teacher told me big legs were great for rowing. That simple link gave me a reason to believe that I could make the rowing team as a sophomore. From there, I built on my reason to believe in being a good rower and became a Navy SEAL. Each one of these successes reinforced my reason to believe that I could handle even harder challenges, such as starting a business. When faced with bankruptcy, I didn't think about going bankrupt; I immediately thought of my reason to believe in NOT going bankrupt. Rowing and SEAL reasons to believe raced through my mind and made me confident that I wasn't going to give up just because the business didn't have enough money. My reason to believe helped encourage my team to find a way to keep the business going.

What's great about recognizing a reason to believe is that it will not only power you during your darkest, most trying times, it will also inspire others to stick with you. Believing in something can be contagious, and when you infect others with a similar reason to believe, you improve your chances of success exponentially. We all want to believe in something, and there's no better person to believe in than yourself. Believe to achieve!

5

few minutes passed as Tim and Peter sat silently enjoying the delectable meal Jacques had prepared. Tim had never tasted anything so exquisite in his entire life; his taste buds were in heaven. He had to keep telling himself to slow down and savor each bite. When a natural opening presented itself between bites, Peter asked, "Well, are you ready for the next action, Skipper?"

"Standing by and ready to receive, sir," Tim responded.

"Okay, so by now you get the importance of believing, right?"

Tim nodded vigorously as he chewed on another mouthful of tuna.

"Good. This next action builds on the other actions; it's all about identifying the obstacles that are preventing you from succeeding. Now, I'm not referring to rocks this time, although these obstacles can be just as stubborn as rocks. I'm referring to the habits you've

Action #5
Survey Your Habits

created either consciously or subconsciously that are sabotaging you." Peter paused for a moment to enjoy another bite of his meal. While he did so, Tim returned to his notepad and drew a thick horizontal line across the page and wrote "Action #5."

"Tim, I alluded to this earlier, but your daily actions form your habits. Habits, the good ones and the bad ones, are nothing more than a sequence of actions that your brain has decided to execute. These habits make up all the actions you take on any given day. The trick is to identify which habits are preventing you from succeeding and to then modify them so they no longer get in your way."

Tim nodded slowly. "Can you give me an example of a good habit and a bad habit?" he asked. "I mean, I think I'm tracking with you, but I'm not sure how a habit can turn a failure into a success."

"Absolutely, and great question," Peter said. "Actually, everyone has a handful of habits that can be, shall we say, re-plotted or reprogrammed. Once that happens, the habits can significantly improve your chances for success. We'll get to that in a minute, but first, an example. Remember when I told you about my first experience of leaving the harbor and how I almost sank from taking on so much water?"

Tim nodded and shuddered. "Yes, the time when you purposely ran your ship up on the rocks?"

The skipper raised his eyebrows and continued, "The one and only. Well, do you know why I took on so much water?"

"You had a hatch open near the waterline?" Tim said hesitantly.

"Not just one hatch; I had four open, and remember that I also lost a bunch of gear, including my tow line."

Tim grimaced at the mere thought of the situation and nodded.

"Well, I lost all that gear and took on water because I had unknowingly created a couple of bad habits, and those habits almost sank me. My bad habits included not immediately latching down a hatch after I had opened it and not tying down a piece of gear after I had used it. I would tell myself, 'I don't have time to latch that hatch or tie that gear right now. I'll do it later.' Well, later would come and go and I would forget all about those things. It all caught up with me when I tried to leave the harbor that

Open hatch

day. The funny thing was, I didn't know I had a bad habit that needed a course correction until a master and commander pointed it out. He said in a salty voice, 'Son, you're never going to get very far if you don't learn to latch a hatch every time you go through it.' He actually made me practice. He wouldn't teach me Action #6 until I latched a hatch one hundred times."

"Come on! He really made you go through a hatch, latch it, and then repeat that one hundred times?" Tim asked skeptically.

"I swear on King Neptune's trident that he did; that old master grabbed a big mug of coffee, perched out on his bridge wing, and counted every single latched hatch. While I was a little annoyed at this simple task, I didn't appreciate what he was doing for me: he was helping me reprogram a bad habit. When I had completed the task, he said, *'The mother of perfection is perfect repetition.'* And you know what? Since that day, I've never left another hatch unlatched."

Peter paused for another bite as Tim wrote down the old salt's saying: *The mother of perfection is perfect repetition.* Tim circled the quote and looked back to Peter to signal he was ready for more.

"Now latching a hatch is an important tactical habit to perform correctly when you're out at sea. I use the word 'tactical' because you need hundreds of tactical habits to keep your ship afloat, such as tying down gear, performing periodic maintenance on your engines, checking seams for leaks — the list goes on. But you need strategic habits to keep your ship on course. It's up to you to decide your course and stick with it. And just like latching a hatch, keeping yourself focused and motivated to stay on your chosen course is a habit — a really important one. The key is to identify those strategic habits that will help you keep your ship on course. This is where exercise comes in; it's not only a good habit, it's also a strategic one."

Tim was fully onboard with the logic of the code and added proudly, "Like making *believing* a habit!"

Peter smiled back and confirmed, "Yes, like making *believing* a habit. It's a very strategic habit."

Tim's confidence had been building throughout the evening. He no longer dreaded the captain's questions; he was catching on.

"But, again, remember that it's easier said than done. I use exercise to help fuel my belief in myself, which serves as the keel, the foundation, to keep me positive. It helps me search for the light in any storm I encounter." As Peter said this, he motioned to the painting that Tim had noticed on his way out to the bridge. "I have this painting hanging right across from where I sit for every meal to remind me that no storm lasts forever. Every storm has its light; you just need to find it. And the way to find that light is to never stop looking. Just like that captain in the painting."

Peter pointed to a figure Tim hadn't noticed before. There was a man dressed in dark greenish-black rain slickers standing proudly behind the helm of his ship. As Tim looked closer, he could just make out a smile on the skipper's face. Tim cocked his head as he discovered the almost obscure feature of the captain in the painting and asked, "Is that a smile on that skipper's face?"

"As a matter of fact, it is," Peter said. "Excellent observation."

"I don't get it; the artist must not have ever been at sea. There's nothing to smile about when you're in a sea like that. Good God, those must be twenty-footers he's up against!" Tim said, his voice rising.

"Actually, the artist *was* the skipper," Peter responded.

"What? C'mon, why would he put a smile on his face? How can anyone smile about being in a storm?" Tim wasn't buying it.

"Well, that's certainly one way to look it at, but what if I told you he was actually looking forward to riding out the storm?"

"I'd say that you and the captain have both lost your compasses," Tim said sharply as he continued to defend his logic. "Who would want to go through a storm?"

"A captain who wanted to know if his improvements to his ship were stormworthy, that's who," Peter said calmly. "That particular artist and captain taught me the code, and, as he explained it, he had created a habit of welcoming adversity. He would say in his gruff voice, 'Peter, always welcome adversity, for there is no better teacher.' He was the single most positive man I have ever met. He was always able to find a light in a storm. I'm quite sure he was smiling when navigating that storm. Want to know why I'm so sure?"

"Yes."

"He was smiling because he was learning," Peter said. "He credited much of his success to the habit he had built over the years to 'never stop learning.' He loved using that phrase." As Peter said these words, he walked over to the painting and motioned to Tim to join him. Peter pointed to a small brass plaque perfectly centered on the painting's gilded frame. Tim quietly read the inscription: *"Prepare for the worst. Expect the best. Take what comes."*

Tim was still having a hard time viewing a storm like the one depicted in the painting as anything but terrifying. Peter picked up on this and continued. "Tim, this captain didn't have a death wish, and this wasn't his first storm. He had weathered many storms prior to tackling this one. And he hadn't been prepared for many of the storms. He would tell me about his white-knuckled fear of facing his first storm outside the relative safety of a harbor. But afterward he remembered how good he felt about riding out that storm. It had given him a sense of accomplishment. He eventually came to appreciate what a storm represents — an opportunity to learn and excel. What would you do and, more importantly, how would you feel if you treated every adversity as an opportunity to excel?"

Peter retreated slowly to the table where the rest of his tuna steak awaited him. Tim kept staring at the painting, his eyes scanning back and forth between that smile on the captain's face and the inscription. He couldn't see one ounce of fear on that captain's face. He was incredulous that any captain would actually welcome the opportunity to take on a storm such as the one depicted in the painting. Tim turned slowly and said, "The storms also served another purpose for that master and commander, didn't they?"

Peter, caught with a mouth full of tuna, responded with a tilt of his head and raised his eyebrows as if to say, "Do tell. . . "

"The storms gave him a reason to believe," Tim said.

The teacher swallowed hastily so he could reward his pupil's remark with resounding encouragement. "Correct! You're catching on! The storm is a symbol of adversity. We will all face adversity throughout our lives; the trick is not to fear it, but to learn from it. And to do this, you must create habits that enable you to keep your mind open to learning new things and to remaining positive so the storm never gets the better of you."

Tim smiled as he returned to his seat to finish what little was left on his plate. The logic of the code was making sense. Each element built on the next, and they all focused on what you can control. And when you can't control something, such as a storm, then do your best to deal with it and learn from it, knowing that when the next storm comes you'll be even better prepared. No wonder that skipper in the painting was smiling. Upon making this connection to the code, Tim said to himself, "I'd smile too if I knew no storm could get the best of me."

The two men sat quietly for a minute, savoring the remaining bites of their meal. Tim wrote down the inscription on the painting while he ate, but modified it slightly to read: "Prepare for the worst, expect the best, take what comes *with a smile.*"

The young captain finished his meal first and asked Peter, "So what other habits did you focus on to help you face adversity and find success?"

"Well, I already mentioned exercise. I believe it's a fundamental, life-changing habit that has many benefits: it gives you strength and stamina to work harder for longer; it makes you healthier so you visit sick bay a lot less often than those who don't exercise; and it's proven to fight depression. The most challenging storms you'll face, Tim, aren't those at sea; they are the ones that occur between your ears — in your mind." Peter sat still for a moment to see if Tim would pick up on his metaphor.

The pupil shifted his gaze toward the fruit bowl centered in the middle of the table and nodded his head slowly while letting the master and commander's words sink in. What Peter was saying was so true. Just twenty-four hours ago, Tim had felt like giving up after hitting that sandbar. He had allowed the put-downs from "friends" like Ted to dictate how he felt about himself. This had made him feel so depressed that he had actually contemplated never leaving his ship again. Then Peter came along and in no time had Tim looking at the positive side of hitting that sandbar. Peter's metaphor made perfect sense. Tim needed to learn to build a habit to keep his mind positive so that no matter what he faced, he wouldn't feel defeated. "I'm tracking with you, Peter," Tim said. "I understand how important it is to keep your mindset positive."

"When I say 'positive,' I'm not talking about being a cheerleader, although sometimes I find that useful too," Peter responded. "I'm talking about having a mindset of always looking for the positive, for what you can learn, in whatever you face. Got it?"

"Loud and clear. So what fundamental habits besides exercise helped you to find success?" Tim was eager to know more.

The seasoned captain smiled at Tim's eagerness and responded, "Why, the code, of course! The more you practice the code, the more you'll appreciate how it will help you succeed by building the habits you need to find success on whatever course you choose. The code is a framework, nothing more. You need to supply the course and the courage. The code will provide a basic plan for going after your dreams, but the effort, the work, and the imagination are up to you. I'm afraid the code is only as good as your willingness to practice it."

"I get it, Peter. I'm tracking with you one hundred percent on this. I'm just wondering if there are other habits I should be aware of." Tim was clearly eager to learn more.

"As a matter of fact, there are other habits you need to be on the lookout for. You need to be ever-vigilant and on guard for habits that will prevent you from going after your chosen courses. Unhealthy habits such as drinking or using drugs can ruin you long before you even leave the harbor. Dishonorable habits such as lying, cheating, or stealing can sink your integrity, and with it your chances of success. We all make mistakes, but when we do, be like the master and commander in the painting." Peter pointed back to the smiling captain facing a twenty-foot wave and said, "And be responsible for your actions by taking them head-on; steer your bow directly toward them and then deal with them. Maintain your course and speed and don't look back. Focus on the next wave."

Tim tried to keep up with his note-taking but found it difficult to write while listening. He nodded as he wrote, a signal to his teacher to keep talking. When Peter paused, Tim asked, "So what do you call Action #5? 'Find bad habits?' "

"Close," Peter said. "I actually call this action 'Survey Your Habits.' You need to build a habit of always watching your actions. Remember, your actions are what make your habits. By creating a habit of surveying your actions, you'll create a safety net for catching a bad habit before it can knock you off course. Make sense?"

"Yes, it does. It makes a whole boatload of sense," confirmed Tim.

"Good, because the remaining three actions are based on Action #5. It's important that you understand that actions are the building blocks of habits, and you're in control of your actions and therefore of your habits. Are you with me?"

"I am, Skipper. Ready to receive your next transmission," Tim said eagerly.

"Very well, Captain Tim. Let's start the next action with a little show and tell, shall we?"

HOW TO GET STARTED

Action #5: Survey Your Habits

SEAL training is divided into three phases, not-so-creatively called the first, second, and third phases. The big challenge in the first phase is Hell-week, and it's responsible for the most voluntary dismissals (quitters) in SEAL training. The second phase includes the Pool Competency Test, aka "Pool Comp," and it's responsible for the most involuntary dismissals (failures). This test includes a series of underwater situations constructed and executed by a team of energetic SEAL instructors. Each situation builds upon the next, with the final one resulting in your loss of the ability to use your scuba tanks. By this time, you've been harassed by up to five SEAL instructors for more than twenty minutes at the bottom of the nine-foot section of the pool. Your adrenalin is pumping, your heart is racing, and you've been gulping air and mouthfuls of water for several minutes by the time your air is cut off completely. Remaining calm is critical; if you don't, you won't be able to hold your breath long enough to complete the required procedures, ditch your dive gear, and pass Pool Comp.

Pool Comp was one evolution I actually looked forward to. I love to scuba dive. I was so excited about learning to do it when I was twelve that I convinced my dad to be my swim buddy and help me get my certification. (This was the youngest age at which our dive shop would certify someone, and I had to have an adult with me.) After I earned my certification, I dove any chance I got. By the time I entered the second phase of SEAL training, I was confident I could pass Pool Comp. I had ten years of diving experience under my belt, and as I found out, ten years of bad diving habits too!

Part of the challenge of SEAL training is being in an environment where nothing is familiar. The uniforms are from the 1940s era, the only swim stroke one can use is unique to the SEALs (called the underwater recovery stroke, it's like a modified side stroke but much faster), the obstacle course is one of a kind, the boats used are relics, and even the exercises are different. Have you ever worked out with a telephone pole? I hadn't. Nor had I ever used the SEAL scuba tanks: two 80-cubic-inch tanks with the first and second stages inconveniently located behind your head and two soft black tubes protruding from the left and right sides of your head. The right tube is for inhaling, and the left one is for exhaling. This dive gear is totally different from the more modern version with a single black hose and the second stage located right in front of your mouth.

Though the gear was different, my confidence remained high. It was still just scuba gear — no big deal. I figured I'd adapt and do what I always did when diving. This was not the right attitude, and worse, the habits I had built over ten years of diving were not the ones the SEAL instructors wanted to instill in us as potential combat divers. I found that out the hard way in Pool Comp.

Pool Comp occurs on a Friday. You get three chances to pass it; two on Friday and one on Monday. My first attempt on Friday morning didn't last more than ninety seconds. Two instructors rolled me, undid my tank straps, and watched me respond. My first action was wrong; I focused on the chest strap, not the shoulder strap. I got the tap on the head to surface, and when I did, I was told to get out of the pool and sit facing away from it so I couldn't see what was happening. That afternoon, I did a little better; I lasted about three-and-a-half minutes before being told to leave the pool. Not good — I had only one opportunity left to pass Pool Comp. Otherwise, I'd be packing my sea bag for a five-year cruise on an "oiler" (a Navy term for a ship that carries fuel for other Navy vessels). That weekend, a veteran SEAL instructor held a remedial class for all of us who had failed Pool Comp twice. Instructor Aloha (obviously not his real name, but he was from Hawaii and was a big-wave surfer with a double dose of Aloha spirit) took a unique approach to prepping us for our last shot at passing the test. The approach had nothing to do with water, which I found unusual, since the entire test takes place in water. Instead, he ran us through a series of drills in the SEAL parking lot that focused on rewiring our bad habits. We weren't failing Pool Comp because of the water; our actions when we were short of breath were preventing us from succeeding. Instructor Aloha said we needed to practice being short of air and perform the correct actions on land before getting back in the water. The drills started with a simple game of hide and seek with some common dive gear: a fin, mask, and snorkel. The instructor named them objects one, two, and three and "hid" them in plain view. The kicker was that we had to collect all three objects on one breath, and there was just enough distance between each one that we had to run to collect all three. At first the game was easy, although we had to pace ourselves through the hide-and-seek course. The drills got more demanding when Instructor Aloha added a pause before telling us to go after the objects so that we would use up more air. In the final phase of the game he changed the sequence for picking up the objects.

One at a time, we would stand at the imaginary starting line holding our breaths as we waited to hear the required pickup sequence—for example, three, one, two. With three objects, the game was relatively simple, but with five the game became a lot more complicated. We had to remember where all five objects were, the number associated with each one, and the sequence in which we were to pick them up, all while starving our brains of oxygen. More than one of us passed out (myself included) while playing his form of hide-and-seek. At first the game didn't make a lot of sense. But by the end, its simple brilliance was sinking in. It was teaching us to think under pressure, or more precisely, to think with limited air!

Once we had all completed the game to Instructor Aloha's satisfaction (which took the better part of Saturday), he numbered the actions necessary for dealing with our diving equipment and had us perform them while holding our breath. We didn't realize it at the time, but he had reprogrammed our bad habits with the good ones required to pass Pool Comp. He had broken down our habits into individual actions, resequenced them while applying pressure (lack of air), and then reinforced them through practice.

The remedial training worked for me. I passed Pool Comp on Monday morning along with the rest of my class. We had an unusually low failure rate, which I credit to Instructor Aloha and his focus on reprogramming bad habits one action at a time.

Pool Comp wasn't the only place where SEAL instructors worked at weeding out and reprogramming bad habits. All of us entered BUD/S with known and unknown bad habits that needed reprogramming. Simple habits such as adjusting dive straps or doing site alignment and trigger control when shooting a gun are easy to identify and correct. For example, when shooting a gun, you either hit or miss the bulls-eye. Once you know what you're doing wrong, an expert marksman can help you break down the building blocks of the successful shooting actions and create a bulls-eye shooting habit. It's more difficult to identify and correct the habits that aren't so measurable, ones such as attitude and attention to detail. Though not nearly as exciting as shooting out the black of a bulls-eye from 200 yards away, attitude and attention to detail are more important to a SEAL officer than having proper site alignment and trigger control. The challenge is to recognize the habits that are blocking you from succeeding. This requires an understanding of what makes a habit.

Whether you're on a journey to lead SEALs into combat, sing on a world stage, or sail the seven seas, the sooner you understand how habits work, the sooner you'll be on your path to success. Habits are nothing more than a specific sequence of actions. Almost every action you take is part of a larger collection. A collection or sequence of actions that, over time, becomes automatic is a habit. The good news is that habits are completely within your control. The trick is to recognize the habit you want to change, identify the actions of that habit, and make the changes necessary to create a new habit. And critical habits can be created even faster. Take opening a parachute, for example. It did not take me twenty-one days to build that habit! *The process for creating good habits is NO different than the one for bad habits.*

There's a simple three-step process for building habits to help you achieve your goal. It's called ACT:

Aware — Be aware of the habit that is holding you back. If you're not sure what it is, ask a friend, teacher, or expert. Be willing to set your ego aside and take an honest look at actions you take for granted. Success is in the details.

Concentrate — Focus on the action or actions that need changing. If you consistently show up late to work or school, then you've developed a habit. Identify the action that's making you late and concentrate on ways to take a new action that will change your habit, such as getting up ten minutes earlier in the morning.

Take control — Once you've evaluated the action that needs to be changed in order to build a habit that helps instead of hinders you, take control of it! Know that any action you generate is your own — you OWN it, and it's within your control. Don't get discouraged; it can take time to change old habits, but it can be done. IT'S UP TO YOU!

As you start to put ACT to use, a funny thing will happen: You'll build a habit of surveying your habits. What better habit is there than one that helps you constantly improve?

To learn more about understanding, identifying, and reprogramming habits, check out *The Power of Habit* by Charles Duhigg—A fantastic read about the power of habits and how they are up to us to harness.

P eter motioned for Tim to join him in leaving the table
as he called out to Jacques and complimented him on a superb meal.
Jacques immediately started clearing the table to prepare it for
dessert. Tim wasn't sure what he looked forward to more, Peter's
show-and-tell or Jacques' dessert dish. The captain of the *Persistence*
informed Jacques that he and Tim would be back in about ten minutes. Jacques responded with a nod as he picked up the plates and
the wooden bowl that had been the centerpiece for the first two
courses and retreated to the galley.

As Tim stood motionless admiring Jacques' efficiency, his teacher
nudged his left shoulder and said, "About face, sailor, I want to show
you a couple of things."

With that they left the warmth of the wardroom and descended
into the belly of the *Persistence*. As they entered the engine room,

Action #6
Improvise

Peter pushed a circular green button located on the starboard side of the room's hatch. Within seconds, a small, muscular man with a well-trimmed beard arrived from behind a bank of batteries. He wore a vest with an assortment of tools stored in pockets across the front. For an engineer, he was remarkably clean — Tim didn't see a single grease mark anywhere on his clothing.

"Captain Tim, it's with great pleasure I introduce you to Robert. He's the one that makes the *Persistence* run flawlessly."

Robert bowed as if he were ducking Captain Peter's compliment. As Tim shook his hand, he grimaced slightly in Robert's iron grip. Tim thought to himself that he really needed to start working out.

"Pleased to meet ya, Cap'n Tim, and welcome to the pride of the *Persistence!*" Robert said with a grin and a wink.

"You got that right," Peter acknowledged. "Robert, we have only a few minutes, but would you mind telling Tim about the battery system you invented for the *Persistence?*"

"With pleasure, Cap'n," responded Robert.

Tim tilted his head toward Captain Peter upon hearing that Robert had invented the battery system. He had assumed that the invention was Peter's. As he turned his attention to Robert, he could not help but admire the cleanliness of the engine room. The young captain had never seen such a tidy one.

Robert pointed out two large banks of batteries and said, "Well, it all started when Captain Peter asked me a question."

"Actually," Peter interrupted, "you asked me the first question."

Robert smiled and offered another wink to the senior captain. "Fair enough, but you would have asked me eventually. I found the captain pacing the boat one afternoon when we re-

Robert

turned from off-loading some cargo. He was so focused on pacing that he almost fell into the cargo hold. I grabbed him and said, 'Yo, Cap'n, what's on your mind?' And that's when he asked me about how we could extend the legs of the *Persistence* to compete with the larger fleet-supported ships. Took some time, but what you're looking at is our solution; a diesel/electric combination that doubled the *Persistence*'s range. Now there's no ocean we can't cross."

Robert raised his chin and with it his chest as he beamed with pride at the accomplishment. Tim couldn't blame him; the system was remarkable. As he stood admiring the batteries and their reduction-gear couplings to the main propeller shafts of the *Persistence*, Peter chimed in. "What Robert is so humbly *not* discussing is that it took more than three years and several dozen prototypes to figure out this system. There were times when I started thinking it just couldn't be done, and he'd grab both my arms and say, 'Nonsense, just need to torture this invention a little more before it confesses to me, Cap'n!' " Peter made the remark while mimicking Robert's thick Irish accent. Tim was stunned to hear that Peter had actually admitted that he considered giving up on something! While Tim was still processing this, Robert said, "Ya know, Tim, I always tell the Cap'n, 'where there's a will there's a way!' And sure enough, we found ourselves a way with this here system. We ain't done yet; got some more modifications to make to her — still learning ya' know — but she's a thing of beauty, ain't she?"

Tim nodded in awe and was surprised at Robert's positive attitude.

If he didn't know better, he would have thought Robert had taught Peter the code!

Captain Peter could see the confusion on Tim's face. It made him chuckle for a moment before he thanked Robert.

"Well, Robert, we'll leave you to implement your latest modification. Thanks for taking a moment to meet Tim, and don't forget to eat dinner. Jacques really outdid himself on this one!"

"I can hardly wait, Cap'n!" Robert exclaimed as he rubbed the tools that covered his lean abdomen, adding with a chuckle, "And Cap'n, make sure you show him my little present!"

"Dessert wouldn't be complete without it!" Peter said. The two of them shared a laugh.

"Nice to meet ya' there, Cap'n Tim. May you have fair winds and following seas, and when you don't, may you never give up." Robert winked as he gripped his hand and shook it vigorously. Tim had to tighten his stomach muscles to absorb the vigor.

Tim nodded dutifully, thanked Robert for his time, and followed his teacher back to the wardroom, where he hoped to get an explanation of what he'd heard below. As they walked into the wardroom, Peter peeked around the corner of his war chest to see if Jacques had dessert waiting on the table. Jacques said from the galley, "When you're ready for dessert, let me know, Captain."

Peter smiled and responded, "Aye, aye, Jacques." Turning to Tim, he said, "He has the best hearing of any person I've ever met. Let's take a seat here for a moment before we have dessert." Peter motioned for Tim to reclaim his chair from earlier in the evening. Before Tim sat down, he went back to the dinner table to retrieve his notepad. As he was returning to his chair, Peter looked up and said, "I bet you have a question or two you'd like to ask me."

"I certainly do!" Tim said passionately. "Did he say you were ready to give up on building the battery system? You, give up? I never thought...."

Peter raised his hand to stop him. "You heard it correctly. I was ready to call it quits on the system. I'm not an engineer, and we had spent *a lot* of money on trying to figure it out. I couldn't afford to spend much more. But Robert, whom I trust with my life, convinced me that he was close; he gave me a reason to believe in him. So I gave him a deadline, Jacques brought him meals around the clock, and he rallied. He worked through nights and weekends until he made it happen."

"So you didn't invent the system?" Tim asked, surprised.

"Absolutely not — Robert did. I merely offered him the support. And in the end, he did two things; he invented it, and he provided me with encouragement to keep believing!" Peter smiled as he reflected on the time it had taken to create the new propulsion system.

"So why was Robert willing to work so hard and so long to create the system?" Tim asked.

Peter's response was instantaneous. "Because he understood the 'why' behind needing this new system. He knew that if the *Persistence* could double its range, we could do some remarkable things."

Tim cut him off. "Such as earn more money?"

Peter nodded and raised his eyebrows slightly. "Sure we'd all make more money, but that wasn't the main driver." As Peter said this he stood up and walked over to the wardroom dining table, where Jacques had returned the fruit bowl minus a few choice pieces of fruit. Peter brought the bowl back to the coffee table.

"No, money wasn't what drove Robert to build the system — it was this." Peter lowered the wooden bowl onto the coffee table and waited for a response.

"Huh? He did it for fruit? Ah, I'm not tracking with you on this one."

"Take a close look at the bowl," ordered Peter.

As Tim focused his attention on the light brown wooden bowl, he realized that the horizontal lines on it were not decorative designs but people's names. He turned the bowl slowly around and looked inside its rim. The names covered the inside and outside surfaces of the bowl. Tim removed a piece of fruit to see how far down the names went. Then he removed another and another, until the entire bowl was empty. He couldn't believe it; there must have been a thousand names on it. Tim looked at his teacher in disbelief.

Peter smiled with pride as he watched his student discover the bowl's uniqueness. "That bowl was given to the crew of the *Persistence* by the chief of the African tribe we delivered food and medical supplies to," he said. "Robert did it for the opportunity to help others; that's what inspired him to make the diesel/electric system."

Tim was speechless.

Peter continued, "We keep it filled with fruit because the chief gave it to us that way and said, 'from this bowl may nourishment always flow for the crew of the *Persistence.*' "

"Is that what those words mean in the bottom of the bowl?" Tim asked, his head nearly inside the bowl.

"I'm sure it's not an exact translation, but yes, that's the drift of those words along with a comment about a tribe of grateful people." Peter waited for just one breath before continuing."Now you know the 'why' behind the propulsion system, but you must understand the 'how' as well. The 'how' is what the sixth action is all about."

Tim put the bowl down and reached for his notepad. He didn't want to miss his teacher's comments.

"Robert didn't create this system overnight. He made several prototypes before he had something we were willing to take to sea. He kept trying different configurations. He wasn't exactly sure what would work and what wouldn't — it took him more than three years of trying to get it right. He improvised, meaning he *implemented, adapted,* and *overcame* each obstacle he encountered." Peter spoke the three verbs deliberately to signal their importance. Tim picked up the signal and wrote the three words down in capital letters on his notepad.

"Every prototype came with its own set of unforeseen obstacles," Peter said. "No sooner did he think he had it solved when another one would pop up. Robert would then adapt and figure out a way to overcome it. What Robert did with the propulsion system is what you need to do when confronted with an obstacle on your course. Implement an action, adapt to the result, and repeat until you've overcome the obstacle. Be like a river and find your path over, under, around, or through — always keep trying and don't stop flowing. Your success will come from your ability to keep trying."

"But even you said you were willing to give up; you were going to let an obstacle stop you," Tim said softly, trying not to be disrespectful to the senior captain.

"Correct, and I'll explain that in a minute. It has to do with the last action. But you have a valid point. I was definitely questioning whether it could be done — no doubt about it." Peter raised his palms as if Tim were a police officer attempting to arrest the master and commander.

Before Tim could probe further, Peter announced, "Jacques, we're ready for dessert!"

"Aye, aye, Captain. It'll be served in sixty seconds," responded the chef.

Peter leaned his head toward the table and said, "C'mon, I want to show you Robert's present — the one he gave me upon completing the system."

Tim grabbed his notebook and jumped to his feet in anticipation. Peter walked Tim past the wardroom table to the port-side porthole and flicked a switch. A small directional light came to life above their heads and illuminated a sculpture made of cables, wires, nuts, bolts, and other oddities. At first Tim didn't get the sculpture — it looked like a mishmash of odds and ends in a recycling bin. He took a step back to look at it from a different perspective.

"Is that a bird?"

"Very good. It is. It's supposed to be a great blue heron, but Robert is no sculptor. Can you make out what it's eating?" Peter asked. That was the one element Tim didn't have a hard time figuring out; it was a frog, and it wasn't just any frog. It was the most muscular frog he had ever seen. Tim chuckled. It was clearly not supposed to look like a real frog; no frog had biceps like this one! Then Tim noticed that the bird had the frog's head in its mouth, but the frog had a firm grasp, with both of its hands, around the skinny neck of the bird. That would explain why the bird's beach-ball-like eyes were nearly popping out of their sockets! Tim laughed out loud as he came to under-stand what the sculpture was depicting.

Robert's sculpture

"Of course Robert made this; look at how ripped that frog is!" Tim exclaimed. Then he noticed the four letters etched in the center of the bronze base of the homemade sculpture: "NEGU." Tim regained his composure and asked, "What does NEGU mean?"

Peter smiled and said, "Why, it's Robert's way of spelling persistence: *'Never Ever Give Up.'* "

They both laughed.

Like clockwork, Jacques arrived holding two decadent desserts, and both men quickly took their seats. Jacques placed a bowl of succulent seasonal berries, slices of star fruit, and hand-churned vanilla ice cream in front of each of them. He left momentarily, only to return with a small ceramic pitcher in one hand and a hand-blown glass bulb in the other. Pouring from the pitcher, he laced their desserts with buttery caramel and then topped them with a sprinkle of sea salt from the bulb in his left hand. Saying nothing, he returned to the galley. The savory dessert needed no explanation.

Both men smiled like kids in a candy store. Lifting his spoon, Peter said, "NEGU is also what the sixth action is all about. Be flexible, improvise and adapt, and keep trying new things until you overcome your obstacle. Got it?"

Peter had beaten Tim to the first bite. Tim put his spoon down, fearing he would later forget his teacher's words of wisdom. As he circled the words "Improvise, Adapt, Overcome" and wrote "Action #6" above them, he made a notation underneath that said, "Be like the frog and never, ever give up — NEGU."

The two sat in relative silence as they raced to finish their dessert before the ice cream melted. Jacques could hear them clanging their spoons in their ceramic bowls as they scraped out the remaining traces of cream and caramel. The noise made him smile.

When the spoon scraping ceased, it was Jacques' cue to clean up and prepare for the breakfast meal. The *Persistence* would be getting underway early the following morning, and Jacques liked to get two meals ahead in case they encountered rough waters after leaving the protection of the harbor.

While Jacques cleared the table, Captain Peter stood up, raised his arms in front of him, and bowed slowly toward Jacques, saying, "Jacques, from beginning to end that was your finest meal yet, my friend. Thank you, and we bow to you!"

Tim scrambled to his feet to imitate the master and commander's gesture of supreme appreciation and said, "Thank you, grandmaster, for the most incredible meal I've ever eaten."

Jacques was touched by Tim's boyish charm and sincerity. He understood why the captain was taking his time in teaching him the code. As far as Jacques was concerned, the oceans needed a lot more captains like Peter. He wondered how much more could be accomplished in the world if there were more leaders like Captain Peter helping others strive to use their talents to the best of their abilities.

Jacques responded with a subtle bow to the captains and remarked, "It has been a pleasure, gentlemen; I'm honored you enjoyed my creations. You'll find refreshments located on the teak table. Goodnight."

The chef's final remarks made Tim pause. Like Robert, Jacques took ownership of his creativity. Though they had totally different responsibilities onboard the *Persistence*, both stressed that they had created things. Robert had created the complex hybrid diesel/electric system, while Jacques had created masterpiece meals three times a day. Tim marveled at how both men took such ownership of their jobs and continually strived to be better. They were never satisfied — they were constantly looking for ways to improve. Then it hit the young captain like a rogue wave: Captain Peter had not only taught the code to future masters and commanders of ships; he had also taught it to his crew. He wanted the crew members to be their own masters and commanders of their jobs. That meant the code wasn't just for future ship captains; it was for anyone who wanted to be better at whatever they did.

Peter was pouring himself a glass of ice water when Tim stumbled on this latest revelation and nearly shouted out, "Peter, the code isn't just for ship captains, is it?"

The wily master and commander turned slowly to face Tim and goaded his pupil into explaining himself further. "Why, whatever would make you think that?" A smirk crossed Peter's face.

"At first, when I watched Jacques work around the table and deliver those divine meals, I thought to myself, 'Wow, Captain Peter's really lucky to have a chef like him.' But then I met Robert, and he paid the same attention to detail and had the same can-do attitude. Both of them made a point of calling out their inventions; they clearly took great pride in their work. I thought with Jacques you got lucky, but once I met Robert I realized that you didn't get lucky, you taught them the code, didn't you?"

"Yes I did, and by the way, bravo for picking up on this — you have excellent powers of observation!" Then Peter said, "I did teach them the code, but it's important to understand that they made the code work for themselves. I can teach anyone the code, but I can't make anyone follow it. That has to come from within. There are many folks out there, like that barge captain you saw earlier today, who couldn't care less about improving or learning. They are quite content just trying to get by in life. As you become more experienced at reading people, you'll be able to tell those who are content to be barge captains for the rest of their lives, and those who want to be like Jacques or Robert or. . . like you."

Peter paused for a moment, took a sip of water, and motioned for Tim to join him back on the ostrich-skin lounge chairs. Then he continued, "The world, the ocean, needs both kinds of people to make it a better place for all. Not everyone wants to be the skipper of the ship and, incidentally, not everyone should be a captain, but for any captain to succeed, he or she needs to be surrounded by a crew that possesses complementary talents. It's not as easy as it sounds; you need to understand what you're good at and what you're not good at — you need to accept that you can't be great at everything." Peter took another sip of water and watched Tim scribble away on his notepad.

"Tim, you need a crew that's great at everything you're not good at, and you need to leave your ego on the pier and be open to accepting that you will not always have the right answer. You'll need to learn to trust your crew. Then a funny thing will happen," Peter said with a faint smile on his lips.

"What? What funny thing will happen?" Tim asked quickly.

"They will trust you. And guess what else will happen?" asked Peter, though he didn't wait for Tim's response. "If you help them be more successful, they will help you be more successful. Simple logic, isn't it?"

"It sure is when you put it that way, but that isn't the way they put it in school. They talk about managing man-hours and how to improve efficiencies. They don't talk about how to trust people or make those who work for you. . . ." Peter interrupted Tim upon hearing the word "for."

"Tim, don't *ever* treat someone as a possession, as a servant — no one works *for* you; you want them to work *with* you. Too many captains on the great blue sea believe their crews are servants, there to do whatever the captain says. This is a flawed mindset. No one who is treated as a servant is going to help you succeed; they are not going to burn the midnight oil figuring out a solution to a ship's problem. Instead, they will spend their extra hours figuring out how to get off the ship. Are you tracking with me on this — never 'for,' ALWAYS 'with' — got it?" Peter was stern with this advice. He knew the distinction was small, but a failure to understand it would have dire consequences.

Tim sat upright as if he were getting dressed down by one of his teachers at school for being disruptive. He nodded slowly and said, "I got it — my apologies — never 'for,' always 'with.'"

Peter returned the nod while locking eyes with his pupil. "As you were saying, Tim...."

"Ah, right, I was saying that school doesn't spend much time teaching us how to manage other...."

"Stop!" Peter exclaimed, as if barking orders to his quartermaster on the helm. "Tim, people like Robert and Jacques don't want to be managed, they want to be led. They want to understand a vision, a 'why' that inspires them, and they want to be a part of the solution that is greater than one's self. To lead is to let go. You must never hover over them and watch the clock. You must get out of their way, arm them with all they need to be the best they can be, and encourage and support them. Help them up when they fall down; praise them in front of the entire world when they succeed. When they go off course, pull them aside without anyone around and discuss a course correction — but whatever you do, *don't try to manage them!*"

Peter took an intentionally long breath to pause for effect and then said, "Have I made myself clear?"

Tim responded sheepishly, "Yes, sir, crystal clear." He wrote down the distinction between manage and lead. He was surprised at how quickly the master and commander's demeanor changed when Tim used the words 'for' and 'manage.' He circled and starred both words in his notes, and then looked up at Peter.

HOW TO GET STARTED

Action #6: Improvise

In the spring of 1997, I deployed with seven other SEALs to Sarajevo on a mission to capture a PIFWC, or Person Indicted For a War Crime. At the time, military operations in Bosnia were considered peace-keeping operations, and the region was divided into segments with different NATO countries responsible for keeping the peace in each one. The frustrating component of this mission was that the PIFWCs were everyday thugs. These men had committed unimaginable crimes against humanity, yet we weren't allowed to conduct direct-action missions to kill or capture them. Our rules of engagement limited us to using roadblocks to capture them, and the men had to be taken alive so they could be tried in the world court at The Hague.

There were seventy-seven PIFWCs listed on a poster in our command post. Each criminal was assigned a number based on order of importance. We were responsible for tracking PIFWC #3, who was wanted on crimes against humanity that included mass genocide. He had been responsible for orchestrating the killing of more than 60,000 men, women, and children. We didn't need a pep talk on the importance of carrying out our mission.

As we prepared, the Army colonel in charge informed me that this particular mission had the attention of a four-star general who wanted command and control over it. I remember commenting to the colonel, "No problem, sir. We'll have Satcom [Satellite] radio with us — he can talk to me anytime." I'll never forget my boss's response: "Lew-Tenant Mills, that's not what he has in mind. He wants to see the whites of this maggot's eyes — you need to send him a picture."

My boss, Colonel Stones (real name withheld), was a decorated Army Ranger with an easygoing Southern drawl who wasn't known for pulling practical jokes, but I couldn't resist asking, "So, we're going to take pictures of the bad guy, send the roll of film to be developed, and wait to hear from the general?" A slight smile formed on Colonel Stones' face as he responded without missing my sarcasm, "Yep, that's just about right except the middle part. You're not gonna send him the roll of film; just one clean picture is all he needs."

Before I could respond, he pulled out a black ruggedized case from underneath his desk and said, "And you're gonna do it with this." What he handed me was a prototype camera of what is now commonly called a digital SLR. Before the colonel let me even touch it, he made me sign for it, all $34,000 of it. I can still hear him telling me, "Now Lew-Tenant, don't be breaking this camera — I'd hate to dock you a year's pay for it."

The camera and laptop we would need to download the pictures presented a real challenge. The mission called for us to spend at least four days deep in the rugged mountains of Bosnia, where we would be close to hostile troops while attempting to take pictures of our target. We spent days preparing for how to use the camera and laptop in a tactical way. From battery life to download and satcom upload practice, we did our best to imagine every conceivable way we might use this technology and how it might fail us. All our practice helped us troubleshoot some critical limitations of the camera and laptop system, such as battery life and durability, or lack thereof. Since we didn't have a local Best Buy where we could get the forty laptop batteries we needed (most shops had been bombed and ruined) or a waterproof bag to protect the system from the elements, we did it the old-fashioned way; we made it. We figured out a way to use the batteries we already had — our satcom radio batteries — and made a one-off neoprene bag from one of our wetsuits to protect the camera. Even with all our prep work, we still missed a limitation that could have cost us the mission.

The autofocus on this first-generation camera was slow—really slow. So every time our target drove by our location, the camera's focus couldn't keep up with the speed of the PIFWC's car. I remember checking in with Colonel Stones and hearing him say, "Mission abort — pictures no good." Our hearts sank; we wanted this guy. We huddled for a couple of minutes, hatched a plan, and responded: "Request twenty-four hours." The colonel granted my request, and we went to work on slowing down the criminal's car. That night we strapped on night-vision goggles, broke out infrared lights, set up an *ad hoc* security perimeter, and went to work digging the perfect pothole. It took two nights to get it just right, and eight more days to get the picture the general wanted, but our improvised plan worked. Within a month, PIFWC #3 was in The Hague, where he would spend the rest of his life answering for the crimes he and others had committed against humanity.

The point of this story is not that there was one less scumbag walking the streets of Bosnia; it's that there was one less scumbag off the streets of this world because of a small team's relentless willingness to improvise when obstacles got in our way. I stress "team" because that's what it took to get past those obstacles, and it was the team's "never give up" attitude that propelled us to improvise again and again until we found mission success. This attitude is not unique to the SEALs. Improvising is a habit like exercising and planning, and it takes time and practice to make it a habit. The ability to improvise is not a talent that you're born with; it's a mindset that you create for yourself. WARNING: This mindset is not a natural attitude; the instinct for most people when presented with an obstacle is to accept it as a limitation and stop all progress. Improvising means more work. It means accepting multiple failures before succeeding. It means doing things differently. Improvising is not normal, but neither is succeeding. Few people succeed at going after their dreams. Those who do succeed do so by willingly taking a different path to get there. You will not find success by doing what everyone else does.

My business partner and I learned this the hard way when we started Perfect Fitness. We worked to find experts to teach us the "right way" to launch our brand on TV. Armed with this information, we raised $1.5 million to create an infomercial to introduce our brand called "BODYREV" to the market. Two-and-a-half years later, we had learned $1,475,000 worth of ways NOT to launch a product. We were down to our last $25,000 before we decided that we needed to improvise and do it quickly.

The hardest thing to accept was that we couldn't get the BODYREV product to work on TV no matter how many different messages we tried. Armed with the knowledge of more than two years of failures, we decided to create an entirely different product. We dusted off my design notebook and picked one I had invented while I was a platoon commander in SEAL Team TWO. With little cash or investor support remaining (some investors told me it was time to stop embarrassing myself and go get a job), we launched Perfect Pushup in the fall of 2006, four-and-a-half years after I had started my journey to build a fitness company. Within two years, our improvised action paid off; we had gone from $500,000 in sales to more than $60 million. Our little company had gained national recognition as the fourth fastest-growing company in the United States in 2009. But no sooner did we think we had success by the reins than we had to improvise again. With the economic downturn of 2008–09, we lost our line of credit from the bank. Without bank support, we couldn't keep shipping to key customers around the nation. We needed to improvise fast or we would go bankrupt.

Twelve months later, we thought we had found a solution to keep us going and growing, only to be forced to improvise for the third time to stave off losing the company. We certainly didn't do everything right, and some of the actions we took along the way didn't help our situation. But we never gave up, and we used our collective ability to improvise and find success.

Along the way of creating what is now more than 40 patented products, I have come to appreciate what I call the three "I's" of Improvise. Not all products are the same, some are completed quickly and simply while others can take years. The key to fast improvising is understanding what kind of improvising you need to do. Before you improvise, ask your self do I need to **I**mprove, **I**nnovate or **I**nvent to succeed at the task at hand? Let's use Perfect Fitness products as the analogy of how to implement the three "I's". The simplest form of improvising is improving something. In the case of Perfect Fitness, over 50% of our products are improvements, such as the Perfect Pushup Stands. We improved the materials (non-slip rubberized grip on the bottom and on the handle), used better resins for a stronger base and changed the designed to give the base more stability hence making it safer. These kinds of improvements took weeks not months or years, but they rarely lead to significant intellectual property protection (i.e. utility patents).

If the situation calls for something more than a simple improvement then it's time to innovate. Our most popular products are innovations. These are products that have a reference point but come with what I call a "surprise" – something that makes you say to yourself, "whoa, I didn't see that coming" – it makes you do a double take. Examples of innovative Perfect products are the Perfect Pushup, the Perfect Pullup and the Perfect Ab Carver. The innovation in these products, or the surprise, is the rotation of the pushup, the adjustable height bar of the pullup and the spring inside the Carver. Critical to the success of the innovation is the logic behind the "why" of the innovation. If you're innovating just to be different and not to really solve a problem then you could be in for real trouble. People will see through your innovation as gimmick, as a "nice-to-have" not a "must-have" which will doom your product to a short lifespan.

By far the most challenging "I" is to invent. Today the verb invent is used loosely to describe any new idea. However, a true invention is an entirely new idea that has no reference point, like the Segway (a two-wheeled gyro-balancing people mover) or in my case, the BODYREV, a rotating weight system. Inventions take lots of time and even more time to educate people once you have built it. (I tell folks to budget three times the length of your development time to educating people on how to use your invention.) About 10% of our time is spent working on inventions at Perfect Fitness. Many times, we will work on inventions knowing they may never come to market only to learn something new along the way that we can apply to other products. Great teams welcome inventions but also appreciate the effectiveness of improvements and innovations.

The scary thing about some improvising is that you have no idea how your idea will turn out. That's okay; no one does. But if you don't try to improvise, your results are guaranteed: nothing. Some of the best advice I received as a SEAL came from my second commanding officer at SEAL Delivery Team TWO. He pulled me aside just before deploying for a special projects mission and said, "Lieutenant Mills, always remember, no matter what happens, make a decision and take action. If it's the wrong decision, you'll know quickly and you can make a better decision. But whatever you do, make a decision — not taking action kills people."

I've never forgotten those words, nor have I forgotten that officer — he was a truly remarkable leader. To improvise is to take action. You won't know if it's the right action until you've ventured down the path of your decision. If it wasn't right, don't allow yourself to get wrapped up in it; just smile to yourself and say, "Okay, I just learned another way NOT to do something," and move on. I've failed many more times than I've succeeded, but those failures have been my building blocks for success. Each failure and subsequent success started with improvising. The key to building an improvising mindset is to create a habit of asking yourself, "Is there a better way to do this?" Seeking a better way, no matter what challenge you face, will lead you to success. Don't wait to ask this question when you're already stuck in a corner. Ask it anytime during your journey that you run across someone making a decision. This could be in a newspaper story, a magazine, a book, the classroom, on a sports field, or on the Internet. The point is that building an improvising mindset happens right now, not just when you need it. Like anything you practice, the more you do it the better you'll get. I'm certain you can find a better way whatever you decide to focus on. Lots of people will come up with a better way to do something, but what will separate you from everyone else is that you're going to take action on your ideas. When an obstacle comes between you and your goal, smile confidently and know that the obstacle is there to stop the other people who don't have the courage or the willingness to improvise around it. You are not like everyone else; you enjoy a good obstacle because conquering obstacles makes you stronger. Not only that, you're prepared because you know the secret to overcoming the obstacle — improvise!

T

he senior skipper looked at his pupil as if he were taking inventory of his vessel before embarking on another course. Tim returned his gaze cautiously after witnessing how quickly his demeanor changed when discussing the differences between leading and managing. The master and commander was clearly passionate about the code and even more passionate about working *with* people to help them achieve their dreams. Tim knew by now that Peter wasn't trying to be mean; he just wanted to make his point crystal clear. Tim waited eagerly to learn the rest of the code. He was ready for Action #7.

The skipper noticed Tim's change in attitude and the way the young skipper's posture straightened as he leaned slightly forward. The more time he spent with Tim, more he was sure that this young man would have the courage to practice the code. Peter cleared his

Action #7
Seek Expert Advice

throat as he prepared to answer Tim's question about Action #7. Just before he spoke, he smiled to himself — he cherished these moments.

"Actually, the distinction between 'manage' and 'lead' has everything to do with the last two actions; seven and eight cover what we just discussed. I'll break it down for you to make it easier to remember, but the essence of Action #7 can be summarized in three thoughts." The master and commander used his fingers to make the three points clear: "First, get comfortable with the fact that you will never be great at everything. Second, understand your talents; know what you're good at and what you're not good at. And third, find people who are great at doing the things you don't do well.

"Remember when I mentioned earlier about leaving your ego on the pier?" Peter said, not expecting a response. "At first it's not easy to do — you're wearing the captain stripes, and you want to have all the answers. But the fact is, you never will, and the sooner you come to grips with this the faster you can start learning from those who have the answers you're missing. That's why Action #7 is called 'Seek Expert Advice.' "

Peter paused for a moment to allow Tim to catch up with his note-taking.

"Robert didn't know the first thing about batteries until he started calling experts from around the world to get an understanding of how he might in-corporate them with the diesel engines he was so familiar with. Same thing with Jacques; when I first met him, he didn't know how to prepare a seafood meal to save his life. That Japanese master and commander who gave me the river rock introduced Jacques to a master sushi chef who taught him an entirely new skill set in preparing raw and cooked seafood. The point is, as soon as you know your weakness, seek the experts that can turn your liabilities into strengths. That's what the seventh action is all about."

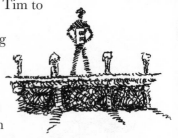

Leave your ego at the pier

The younger captain nodded yet again at the master and com-mander's sage advice. As he exhaled, he let a half-chuckle escape, which prompted his teacher to ask, "What's so amusing, Tim?"

"I just realized that I'm already practicing Action #7; I'm here seeking *your* expert advice," he said with a smile.

"Very good point, and, I might add, you've been an excellent stu-dent thus far. We have only one action left, my friend, and then the real test comes," said Peter. For the first time in the past two hours, Tim got another of those uneasy feelings. He fidgeted nervously in his chair and said, "Ah, okay, anything I should know before learning the next action—you know, so I can be prepared for it?"

"Nope, no need to worry about it; it's just your final exam for un-derstanding the code," Peter said nonchalantly as he watched Tim squirm in his seat. Then he heard him exclaim, "Final exam! You didn't tell me there was a final exam on the code!"

HOW TO GET STARTED

Action #7: Seek Expert Advice

There's nothing unusual about Action #7. It defines exactly what needs to be done: seek expert advice. It was the first action we always took as SEALs after learning about a mission assignment. It was also the first action we took after deciding what kind of product we wanted to launch at Perfect Fitness. The premise is simple: *Learn from those who have gone before you.*

If you search carefully and ask thoughtfully and politely, you can almost always find someone willing to share words of wisdom that can help you improve your chances of success. Depending on your goal and the value of the wise person's advice, you may have to offer something more than a thank-you note for compensation (money or stock, for example), but the right expert can shave hundreds if not thousands of hours of frustration and false starts off your journey toward achieving your goal.

The challenge with Action #7 comes from within — it's called ego. We humans love to think we know it all. We can be bold in our thinking, yet backward in our approach to following up on an idea. Pick up a newspaper or read the front page of a news website and you'll find examples of people failing spectacularly because they didn't ask for advice from someone who had journeyed down a path similar to theirs. Seeking an expert is no different from asking a teacher for help in solving a homework problem. Depending on the size and boldness of your goal, you may have to find multiple experts to help you chart a course to success. You will never know it all, and the sooner you come to grips with this concept, the faster you can get on your path to fulfilling your dreams.

JO's, or junior officers, have only a short time upon arriving for SEAL duty to earn the respect of their platoon mates. This can be a critical milestone in building a reputation as an officer others would join in going into combat. Arriving with a college education and a certificate of completion from BUD/S doesn't get you respect; it merely gets you through the front door for consideration for a leadership position. The ability to ask others for advice is more important than diplomas, marksmanship awards, or how many push-ups you can do. The others I'm referring to are the men that technically report to you. They have years more experience than you'll ever have as a SEAL. This is one of the great paradoxes of military command: Those in charge often have the least experience.

A JO's SEAL career can be an extremely short one if he doesn't admit that he doesn't know nearly as much as he thinks he does. I was no different from any other JO in my position. I was excited to get to work and eager to earn the respect of the veteran SEALs. Thankfully, two warrant officers took me and another JO under their supervision and taught us the importance of learning from others. These two officers were my experts. They taught me and my swim buddy everything we needed to know to survive and thrive while driving a classified combat mini-submersible called a SEAL Delivery Vehicle. I'm certain that without those two warrant officers, my SEAL career would have taken a very different path. On more occasions than I care to count, the teachings of those two experts saved my life and the lives of others. I admit I didn't always ask them for advice. Instead I believed I had mastered what they had taught me. Every time I felt that way — every time I became a little too arrogant — I would make a mistake. The officers often reminded us that "arrogance kills." Unfortunately, the SEAL team is not bulletproof to this mindset. There have been plenty of times throughout the team's storied history when an officer in charge has allowed his arrogance, or ego, to get in the way of asking for advice from experts. Such arrogance has often led to injury or death.

While this may be an extreme example of what can go wrong when you don't seek expert advice, the point remains: *You will never know it all. Use experts to help you excel.* Every time I embark on a new goal I do three things:

1. Define the goal and make it as measurable as possible.

2. Define my "why" — why is this goal worth focusing on and why is it worth dedicating time to?

3. Decide who can help me get started on the goal.

Be prepared to seek out a variety of experts. There will be experts to help get you started, some to help get you unstuck, and others to help get you across the goal line. I categorize experts into a simple acronym I call "S.E.T." as in *Get SET!* like you are about to start a race (which by the way, you kind of are beginning a race, a journey race that is, when you have decided to get out of your comfort zone!). There are three kinds of experts that you will need in life: Strategic, Emergency and Tactical experts. Sometimes one expert can play multiple roles, like a Dad being both a Strategic and Emergency expert. But as your dreams get bigger and bolder, your "S.E.T." team does as well.

Some might be able to help throughout the entire journey toward your goal, but those are rare. When I started Perfect Fitness, I sought out experts in operations, finance, industrial design, marketing, infomercials, sales, e-commerce, human resources, banking, accounting, legal issues, and more. I cannot stress this enough: You will need help, so get comfortable asking for it. This can be your biggest asset or your biggest liability. The better your experts the better your chances for success. The sooner you become willing to seek out experts for assistance, the faster you'll achieve your goal. *Put your pride aside: seek expert advice!*

People often ask how I invented the Perfect Pushup. The short answer is that I invented the Perfect Pushup along with about twenty-five other people. Sure, I came up with the idea, but an idea isn't worth the napkin it's printed on without others, including some who know more than you do, helping you make that idea a reality. You may also convince many of these experts to join you on your journey, which is what the eighth and final action is all about.

The master laughed and said, "Why, of course there's a final exam; how else are you going to truly learn the code?" Peter grinned from ear to ear as he watched Tim flip his notes nervously back and forth in a weak-hearted attempt to cram for the exam. The sly captain didn't want the remaining action to receive any less attention than the other seven, so he tried to put Tim at ease. "Tim, there's nothing to worry about; it's a take-home exam. Now put your pencil down and pay attention to the last action."

Tim took a deep breath, put his pencil across his notepad, and leaned back to soak in the precious time he had left with this remarkable captain. "I'm all ears, Skipper," he said, his relief obvious on his face.

"Excellent. Now let's go back to the basics. Remember when we discussed how some courses you choose will require more effort than

Action #8
Team Up

others?" asked Peter, leaning forward and resting his forearms just above his knees.

"Yes I do. You said no two courses are alike. Some will be easier and some will be harder," Tim answered in textbook fashion.

"Perfect — you're dead-on. Action #8 is about those courses you choose in life that are a true challenge for you; the kind that scare the hell out of you and leave you wondering, how on earth am I going to accomplish this?" Peter spoke with an assurance that made it sound like a guarantee that Tim would one day pick a much less traveled course — and that thought alone made him queasy.

"Tim, the tougher the course, the more rewarding it will be. I promise, it will be worth it. But you won't be able to do it alone. As your confidence grows from one slightly bigger course to the next, there will come a time when you'll opt for a course that's not just a bit more challenging, but *a lot* more challenging — like when I wanted to steam across an entire ocean. I didn't have a clue how to do it, but do you know how I figured it out?"

This time Peter waited for an answer. His student thought for a good twenty seconds before blurting out, "You used Action #7!"

The master and commander took pride in his student's response; he was pleased at how quickly this young captain had taken to understanding the code. "Correct! I started by asking people who had already done it. I sought expert advice, and you know what they told me? Every single one of them?" Peter went quiet as he waited for a response.

Tim took his time on this question; the weight of having just answered the last one correctly pushed down on him. He wanted to make sure he kept his streak of correct answers going. "That you couldn't do it alone?" Tim's response was more like a question than an answer, but Peter didn't care. The code was clicking, and he wanted to give Tim as much encouragement as possible, for this could be the last time the two of them would ever see each other, though he truly hoped that wouldn't be the case.

"*Yes!* Exactly, Tim! All these wise old captains said, 'Son, don't be foolish. Crossing an ocean in a boat like yours requires the help of more than just one person, and not just any kind of person; you need a crew that is competent and confident,' " Peter said excitedly. "That search led me to find Robert and Jacques, and thank goodness I listened to their wise words. Now, I admit, I had already learned the code, but these old salts reinforced the importance of Action #8 — I needed to *team up* with other people who were great at the things I wasn't great at. Get it? After you *seek expert advice,* go out and build a team that supports what you've learned from your experts. And, Tim, how are you going to attract the right team for your course? It has to do with Action #1," Peter said with a wink.

"Oh, I gotcha! I'm going to find teammates who are as inspired with my 'why' as I am!" Tim said. "So wait, that means I'll be repeating the code again, but this time I'll be doing it with more people following the actions with me! I get it; it's a never-ending cycle. Once I've accomplished something, I put the code to work again on a bigger course, and as the courses demand more people, the code can be applied to a team. But it all starts with figuring out the why." Tim's words came faster as the logic of the code became clearer. He continued, "And when you have a team, you all work together to figure out the way." Tim's voice drifted off for a moment as he came to another realization. "Which means you can cover more courses faster if you have the right team, and you can accomplish so much more if your team all believes in the 'why.' And it's your team that helps you figure out the 'way!' " Tim jumped to his feet, made a fist with his right hand, and smacked it into his left palm while letting out a yelp of delight — he understood the logic of the code. He now saw how the actions connected and could be applied on a much broader scale. His mind raced with this newfound knowledge. Captain Tim would never be the same. He was already thinking differently. He was inspired to dream big.

As the young captain jumped around the wardroom, he noticed more artifacts of all shapes and sizes. He bet each one represented some component of a dream Captain Peter had navigated. He was anxious to get going on his own courses, collect his own mementos; he wanted to build his own war chest of keepsakes.

The master and commander smiled proudly as he watched the lights go on inside his pupil's head. He relished this moment. It never got old for him — helping the next generation see their potential. He wished he could be alongside each and every one he'd ever taught the code to; he wanted to cheer them on when they stumbled, encourage them when the wind, waves, and water were working against them and, most of all, he wanted to be there to celebrate their successes. He knew that was unrealistic, for the code's very premise was that his students would have to discover their course for themselves. He couldn't do that for them, any more than he could do their navigating — it was up to them. Instead he'd created a keepsake that he gave to each student to whom he'd taught the code. And now was the time to award Tim with his first master and commander memento.

The young captain was so busy pacing back and forth and repeating the code over and over in his head that he didn't notice his teacher opening up the bottom shelf of his war chest and removing a miniature paddle.

Peter cleared his throat and stood across from Tim, whose back was still turned, and said, "Tim, the time has come, my friend."

As much as he hoped the evening would last for an eternity, Tim knew he'd be leaving shortly; still it was hard to hear the words. His heart sank ever so slightly. He had never spent an evening like this — it had been a life-changing experience. When Tim turned to face the master and commander, he saw Peter standing with his arms outstretched, holding a beautiful small paddle in his hands. The wood glistened under the wardroom light.

"Tim, this is for you. It's more than a memento of our evening; it's a checklist and constant reminder of what it takes to be a master and commander," Peter said proudly while offering the gift to his student.

Tim's mouth was agape. The evening had already been more than he could ever have imagined. But this wasn't a paddle; it was a work of art and a tool of inspiration all wrapped into one.

"Go ahead and read it," encouraged Peter.

The young captain was still speechless as he gingerly held the paddle and scanned it from handle to blade tip. There were letters and words inscribed on the handle, stem, and blade. Tim looked closer and

A memento

saw that it read "U-PERSIST" from the handle down the stem. On the blade was the quotation from the compass on the master and commander's helm: *"Nothing in the world can take the place of persistence. Talent will not; nothing is more common than unsuccessful men with talent. Genius will not; unrewarded genius is almost a proverb. Education will not; the world is full of educated derelicts. Persistence and determination alone are omnipotent. The slogan 'Press On' has solved and always will solve the problems of the human race."* At the very bottom were the letters N E G U, clearly carved by someone else's hand. Tim smiled; he bet those letters were Robert's handiwork.

Peter cleared his throat again; he always found himself getting a little emotional when presenting a paddle to one of his students. He hoped it would be of use when they ventured on their own course. Perhaps it would provide them with inspiration when doubt crept in. How he wished he could be there to whisper in their ears to keep going. The paddle was his way of being there for his students; it was his whisper of inspiration.

"Tim, it is with great honor that I bestow upon you this master and commander paddle. It symbolizes the earliest form of propulsion. Before there were propellers, sails, steam engines, diesels, and electric motors, there was the paddle. The earliest captains followed their courses using a paddle. So I thought it only appropriate to use it as the platform on which to inscribe the code and its meaning."

Captain Peter pointed to the persistence quotation below and then said with a wink and a smile, "And Robert's definition, too — *Never, Ever Give Up.*"

The student nodded enthusiastically at his teacher's comments but did a double-take when it came to the letters inscribed on the paddle from the handle to the stem. Peter caught his confusion and re-marked, "Tim, those are the first letters of each of the eight actions of the code, and they represent what you must do to navigate your course successfully: U-PERSIST."

The younger captain started repeating aloud each of the actions; he hadn't put them together until that moment, but now he saw that they spelled out what he was supposed to do!

Captain Peter heard him recite the code. "U — Understand; P — Plan; E — Exercise; R — Recognize; S — Survey; I — Improvise; S — Seek; T — Team up. It's brilliant! I wondered how I was going to remember all eight actions," exclaimed Tim.

"There's beauty in simplicity, my friend," Peter said. "The code is simple, and I've put it into a framework that's easy to remember. However, putting it to use will be up to you, and you alone. I hope this paddle will serve as a constant reminder that you are limited by only two things in your life: your ability to dream and the courage to pursue those dreams. There's an amazing world waiting for you out-side this harbor." Peter pointed toward the bow of the *Persistence*, which was aimed toward the bay of Hardwork Harbor. "You have the boat and brains to explore the world. All you need to do now is to find a course and have the courage to follow it."

Peter paused for emphasis and moved closer to Tim as he said, "Tim, the wind, waves, and water can work for you or against you — they can kill you or transport you. It's *up to you* how you handle their forces. At times they will seem like nothing but obstacles, and when they do, smile and learn from them, because the *obstacle is your course*. Never stop learning, especially when presented with adversity. Remember, your brain is only as good as the inputs it receives — spend your life filling it with new inputs that will help you dream up new courses to conquer. Your life is Up To You!" As Peter said these final words, he grabbed Tim's biceps and squeezed them firmly while staring intensely into his eyes. He wanted to make sure Tim understood that his life and the courses he would choose were en-tirely up to him.

The young captain looked down toward the paddle, but he wasn't really looking at it. He couldn't hold back a few tears of joy, sadness, and thanks for what Captain Peter had given him that evening. Ever since he had left home for school, no one had taken a special interest in him the way Peter had. The master and commander had filled him full of hope, encouragement, and inspiration. He felt ready to conquer the world, and he didn't have the slightest idea how to thank this magnificent teacher. All he could do was bow his head while trying to clear the growing lump in his throat.

Tim mustered up a muffled "thank you" and wiped away the tears as the paddle and its inspirational words came back into focus. The teacher smiled proudly at his new star student, and said, "Turn the paddle over; there's a cheat sheet on the back, and one more quote just to make sure you never forget what the code is all about." The grateful captain turned the paddle over and read what the master and commander was referring to. On the back of the blade was the following inscription:

Understand the why, and you'll figure out the way
Plan in three dimensions
Exercise to execute
Recognize your reason to believe
Survey your habits
Improvise to overcome
Seek expert advice
Team up
"Before the gates of excellence, the high gods have placed sweat."

The Peter could feel his pupil's appreciation; he didn't need to hear a word. His student's reaction was his reward. He gave him a big bear hug. As he did so, he said, "From here on out, Captain, face forward and always point your bow out to sea. It's not about where you've been; it's about where you're going."

Tim nodded silently to acknowledge the remarks. As he was collecting himself to go ashore, Captain Peter left him with one more thing to think about it, "Speaking of 'going' places, should you ever feel inspired to leave the harbor, may I suggest charting a course to the harbor of the Big Island in the BYIs – seek the Harbor Master."

Tim's mind and emotions were racing as he heard yet another riddle of sorts from his teacher. He wanted to stay and ask more questions, he wasn't ready to leave, but he knew it was time. Peter said with a wily smile, "Time to go ashore, shipmate!"

As the two captains walked down the gangplank of the *Persistence*, Tim desperately wanted to ask about his teacher's last riddle. "Who's the Harbor Master"? "Where are the BYIs"? And, most importantly, "What would he learn there?" As these questions bounced inside the young skipper's head, he failed to notice that Captain Peter stopped just short of leaving the gangplank. Tim was clutching his notebook in his left hand and the paddle in his right when he realized he was alone. He quickly turned to get one more look at the remarkable vessel and its captain. The master and commander stood proudly on the last rung of the extended gangplank of the Persistence and performed a crisp right-handed salute. As he did so, he spoke in a voice Tim hadn't heard all evening; it was that of a captain giving a command: "Full speed ahead, Captain. Your course awaits. Work hard, have fun, and never, ever give up. And always remember where you came from. Your life is Up To You!

Tim didn't fall asleep until well after four bells sounded on his ship's chronometer. His mind was in high gear, processing the evening he'd just experienced on the Persistence. His thoughts darted from reciting the eight actions of the Master and Commander Code to the conversations he had with Robert, Jacques, and of course Captain Peter. Then there was that meal onboard the Persistence — he wanted to savor it all over again. And while he thought about each mouthful of Jacques' remarkable creations, his mind drifted to all the artifacts and mementos Peter had collected. He wondered if any of them were related to his last comments about the Big Island, the BYIs and the Harbor Master. Tim even thought about where he would display the mementos he would collect from his own adventures. At one point, while he tossed and turned in his bunk, he thought about measuring a space in his cramped wardroom where he could build his own war chest. As drowsiness finally calmed his mind, Tim's last thoughts were about which course he should focus on next.

Tim didn't fall asleep until well after four bells sounded on his ship's chronometer. His mind was in high gear, processing the evening he'd just experienced on the *Persistence*. His thoughts darted from reciting the eight actions of the Master and Commander Code to the conversations he had with Robert, Jacques, and of course Captain Peter. Then there was that meal onboard the *Persistence* — he wanted to savor it all over again. And while he thought about each mouthful of Jacques' remarkable creations, his mind drifted to all the artifacts and mementos Peter had collected. Tim wondered where he would display the mementos he would collect from his own adventures. At one point, while he tossed and turned in his bunk, he thought about measuring a space in his cramped wardroom where he could build his own war chest. As sleep finally calmed his mind, Tim's last thoughts were about which course he should focus on next.

One prolonged blast on a departing ship's whistle nudged Tim awake. It took more than a minute for him to take in his surroundings. He had slept so soundly that he was disoriented. It wasn't that he didn't know his own room; that wasn't the cause of his disorientation. He was wondering if his evening with Captain Peter had really taken place or if it had been merely a dream. He felt a pit in his stomach as he began to think that his dinner on the *Persistence* was nothing but a figment of his imagination. He bolted to the nearest porthole to see if the grand vessel was moored where he thought it should be, directly off his bow. As he squinted in the morning sun reflecting off the glassy water, the pit in his stomach doubled in size; Tim saw nothing but an empty mooring ahead of his ship. Captain Peter and the *Persistence* were gone.

Then he remembered the paddle; where had he put the paddle from last night? If he could find that, he would know for certain that it had not been a dream. He did a quick scan of his room — no paddle. The pit in his stomach started to burn. He raced through his galley and miniature wardroom — again, no paddle. Now he was frantic. He ran to the bridge and there, perched above his compass with the handle facing the bulkhead, was the master and commander paddle!

Tim smiled and laughed at himself for thinking that the conversations and the meal the night before had been a dream. He picked up the paddle and examined it closely, as if making sure the engraved code was still there. Satisfied that it was exactly as he remembered it, Tim searched for some heavy-duty tape so he could secure the paddle directly above the compass. Until he could craft some brass brackets, it would have to do. He wanted it prominently displayed on the bridge so he would be constantly reminded of the code and Captain Peter. As he taped the paddle to the bulkhead above the compass, a radio transmission interrupted his thoughts. "Calling Captain Tim, Calling Captain Tim, this is Captain Bill, please report your status and your Echo Tango Alpha, over."

The words hit Tim like a bucket of ice water. He nearly dropped the paddle as he scrambled to collect his thoughts and return the radio request. He had totally forgotten that he had to steam back across the bay today. The pit in his stomach returned. He hastily finished taping the paddle above the compass and replied to Captain Bill's radio request with little enthusiasm: "Cap'n Bill, this is Cap'n Tim. I read you loud and clear — will be underway shortly." Tim paused momentarily to run a quick estimated time of arrival calculation in his head and said, "Expect to arrive at 1600 hours...BREAK...belay my last — Echo Tango Alpha — 1600 hours — over."

Captain Bill responded almost instantaneously with, "Roger, copy all Captain Tim — I will be monitoring Channel 72 should you need assistance. Transit safely. Captain Bill out."

As much as Tim wanted to stay on the bridge and daydream about the previous night, he couldn't. He had overslept and needed to get his ship underway. There was a lot to do and not much time to get it all done if he was going to have any chance of making it home by 1600 hours.

Tim checked out with the repair crew, certified that all cargo had been properly off-loaded, went through his normal underway checklist, and did final preparations to steam back across the bay. The pier-side line handlers shouted in perfect unison, "All clear, Skipper!" Tim gave one prolonged blast on the ship's whistle to let everyone know he was underway. As he steered a reciprocal course back to the south side of Hardwork Harbor, he didn't feel the same nervousness in his belly that he'd felt the day before. He had found strength from Captain Peter's words. He replayed the portion of the conversation from two nights ago when the captain had regaled him with stories of running aground all over the world. Tim could hear the master and commander's words: "Tim, my attitude is, if you don't run aground from time to time then you're not trying hard enough. The way I see it, Tim, the important thing about running aground is making sure you understand *why* you ran aground."

The young skipper knew exactly why and where he had run aground two days ago. He smiled as he said out loud to himself, "Not this time, Buoys 15 and 17 — you two are on my chart now." Tim's journey home went without incident, and he arrived fifteen minutes earlier than he had predicted. He had been so focused on navigating that he didn't hear the snide remarks on the radio from Ted and his little fleet of so-called friends.

Tim returned a different captain, and Ted sensed it after watching how Tim responded to him on the pier. Ted called out and said, "Hey Captain Sandbar, how was the trip across the bay?" Ted's comment earned him a few chuckles from the other young captains hanging with him on the pier. Tim smiled and stood a little taller as he turned to Ted and said, "It was fantastic! Thanks for asking; can't wait to do it again." The vigor of his response startled Ted and caught the attention of Captain Bill, who was waiting to debrief Tim on his voyage. Before Ted could muster a response, Tim turned to the senior captain of the cargo fleet and said, "Cap'n Bill, I'd like to share with you what I learned. Where would you like to conduct the debrief, sir?" The elder skipper smiled and said, "Sounds good to me, skipper. How about giving me the download on the quarterdeck with the other captains who are due to run the course tomorrow?"

"Aye, aye, Cap'n," responded Tim as he turned away, leaving Ted and his small fleet of followers speechless on the dock. Ted hadn't expected Tim to be so positive after returning from a voyage that Ted clearly thought was a failure. Ted could tell Tim was different. He couldn't put his finger on it, but Tim seemed more confident — he held his head high. Normally when Ted made fun of him, Tim would drop his chin to his chest and roll his shoulders forward, acting like the loser Ted expected him to be. Ted couldn't figure it out. His comment about Captain Sandbar seemed to have the opposite effect on Tim. Ted actually thought Tim looked taller than he remembered. Ted didn't get it, and since he didn't get it, he reverted to what he knew best, which was making fun of Tim behind his back. He said his next remark just loud enough for Tim to hear. "Look, fellas, there goes the first one in our class to run his ship aground. Maybe he ought to go back to Navigation 101!" Ted's friends chuckled at his joke, but not as heartily as Ted had expected.

While Ted was busy trying to keep his friends focused on making fun of Tim over the coming weeks, Tim earned a spot on the cargo fleet's weekly rotation to navigate to the north side of Hardwork Harbor. He visited Cap'n Jack's Clam Shack as often as his schedule permitted, and always secretly hoped to find Captain Peter sitting at the helmsman's table. As the weeks turned into months, Tim learned new courses that eventually took him to every port in and around Hardwork Harbor. Along the way, the skipper kept a log of what he learned on each new course. Over time, he made more modifications to his ship, such as widening his cargo bays to carry bigger loads and installing ramps to handle different kinds of goods. But one modification he made changed his course forever. It wasn't so much the modification itself as it was the confidence he gained from proving his idea worked.

He hadn't run aground since that first course heading North in Hardwork Harbor, but he certainly hadn't forgotten it. Running aground had scared Tim. Every time he was underway he would think of running aground; it haunted him in his dreams and made him throttle back when he could have completed his courses faster. The fear had a hold on him — it limited him. As much as he wanted to be like Captain Peter and chart courses outside Hardwork Harbor, he just couldn't get past the thought of running aground. One sleepless night, as Tim was preparing for another course across Hardwork Harbor, a thought came to him on how to deal with his fear. "If I can't get rid of my fear of running aground, why not create something to be my shield against it?" That night a slew of crazy ideas meandered through his head, from extending long metal sensors under the bow of his ship to affixing bulldozer tracks to the bottom of his ship so he could drive over sandbars. One night led to several nights, which led to working on weekends to figure out a solution to his phobia of running aground.

His ultimate solution was simple: He'd build a metal cage around his propeller, because that was what had been damaged and prevented him from getting off the sandbar the first time. He figured if he could prevent his propeller from getting damaged, he could get his ship off most obstacles. Suddenly, and strangely, Tim's fear of running aground wasn't so debilitating. He actually looked forward to finding out if his idea would work; running aground was turning into a problem to be solved instead of something that prevented him from doing what he wanted. Once Tim installed the cage-like covering, he looked for a sandbar to run aground on. When he finally got his chance to test out his new idea, he thought about Captain Peter's painting of the smiling captain head-

Captain Tim's solution

ing into the storm. Less than a year after meeting the master and commander, Tim was looking for his own storm to conquer, and his storm to conquer was his ship running aground. He smiled as he headed out of port in search of a sandbar. He knew just where to go: between buoys 15 and 17. He throttled back just to be safe, spun the helm to right full rudder, and gently ran his ship up on the sandbar.

"What a difference an attitude can make," Tim said aloud as his vessel ground to a stop on the sandy bottom. He took a deep breath, looked at Persistent Pete's paddle, smiled, and put his ship into reverse. For a few nervous seconds nothing happened — then, progress! He felt it before he saw it. The device was working! As the propeller dug into the water, the stern sank briefly before the cage met the edge of the sandbar. With the propeller protected, it was able to provide enough reverse thrust to pull Tim's ship off the sandbar. Tim held his breath for what seemed like an eternity before his boat began to reverse course. He yelled at the top of his lungs: "Yes! Yes! Yes! It worked! I did it!" He did a little celebratory dance on the bridge before throttling back the engine and heading back to port. From that moment on, the pace of Tim's ship modifications quickened. He tried all kinds of experiments. Some worked and lots of them didn't, but none of the experimenting slowed him down. As he spent more time dreaming up new things to do to his ship, the idea of tracking and logging work hours became lost on Captain Tim. No longer did he feel the pressure to be on time for work at 8 a.m., nor did he count down the hours until 5 p.m. when the workday was over. Tim woke up early to get to his ship and stayed late into the night, not minding what time it was. His work attitude was transforming from the mindset among others in the fleet of "work to live" to the master and commander's "live to work."

The confidence Tim gained from overcoming his fear of running aground led him to dream bigger — much bigger. He was ready to turn his next dream into a new course. He wanted to take a route out of Hardwork Harbor.

Tim's course out of the bay had started when he answered Captain Peter's question concerning what he was willing to give up to follow his own dreams, his own courses. His confidence and courage to follow his course out of Hardwork Harbor didn't grow overnight. It took Captain Tim more than two years of planning after that evening on the *Persistence* with Captain Peter learning the Master and Commander Code. He spent countless hours over late nights and weekends, trying to understand the obstacles that prevented him from going after his own course. He knew that if he did only what the fleet required of him, he would never leave the bay. He learned that to achieve his freedom to follow his own course, he would have to do more. He would have to put forth more effort than what was expected of him by friends, family, and his senior captains. He realized if he wanted an extraordinary life, he'd first have to make extraordinary sacrifices. He had to work harder, think differently, and not be afraid to stand out from the other captains in the fleet. He came to accept failure as a rite of passage on his course to following his dreams. He became comfortable confronting his fears — accepting that it was okay to be afraid, but that it was up to him not to let his fears control his course.

Tim hadn't realized it at the time, but all his actions since meeting Captain Peter had put him on a master and commander's course. The young skipper would often fall asleep wondering what his life would be like when he was a master and commander; he was thinking of it as a destination. What he didn't realize was that he'd already become a master and commander when he decided to try a little harder and work a little longer each day to pursue his own course. What Captain Peter didn't tell Tim was that when you follow your own course and the code, you become your own master and commander.

The other little detail Captain Peter kept from the young skipper was a rule that prolonged Captain Tim's departure from Hardwork Harbor for one day. On the morning Captain Tim alerted Captain Bill that he was getting underway, the elder captain asked, "do you have your courses plotted Tim?" the young skipper responded proudly, "Yes sir, plotted and doubled checked." Bill smiled back at him and said, "Good – where ya headin' to Capt'n?" Without missing a beat, Tim replied with excitement: "to the Big Island of the BYI's". The senior sailor nodded slowly while keeping a smile on his face and said, "I'm sorry, Tim; you can't leave today."

Incredulous, Tim responded, "Why not? I'm ready!" "I know you are, but your ship isn't," replied the seasoned fleet captain. "You need a name for your ship — it's an international maritime law." He chuckled and said, "One more day won't keep you from following your course, Tim. Name your ship proudly. And may you have fair winds and following seas, and when you don't, may you never ever give up." Tim stood there, thunderstruck at the captain's remarks. Before he could respond, Captain Bill said "oh, and one more thing, when you get to the Big Island, please give the Harbor Master a salute from me."

Tim's eyes nearly popped out of his sockets upon hearing the senior skipper's request. He sounded just like Captain Peter! Captain Bill, the one who had been there for him when he first ran aground; the one who was always the first to offer assistance; the one who was always interested in what Tim had learned from his courses across the bay. Was he a master and commander, too? And how did he know about the Harbor Master? Tim couldn't get those thoughts out of his head while spent the rest of the day determining what he should name his ship. As he paced the bridge pondering the perfect name, he kept looking at the paddle Captain Pete had given him and remembering all that it represented. As the sun set to the west over Hardwork Harbor and Tim watched the last rays of light fight their

Captain Tim

way through the trees and ships that dotted the shoreline, a name came to him. He spent the evening with a woodworker he knew and helped carve it into three planks of teak. When he was finished, Tim used brass screws to affix a plank on either side of the bridge and the third one to the transom. Now he was ready to leave the bay and follow his own course, a course that he charted to the BYIs.

The next morning, Tim was up early double-checking his ship to ensure everything was ready for his course out of the bay. As Tim was
finishing up, Captain Bill and a couple of other senior captains of the
fleet came by to see him off. They handled the dock lines as Tim ma-
neuvered his vessel away from the pier. As he blew his ship's whistle for
one prolonged blast to signify that he was underway, the captains on
shore came to attention and saluted. Tim was surprised that anyone
had showed up, let alone Captain Bill, and as he marveled at the
crowd, he heard Captain Bill's reassuring voice boom out over the water: "Live by your ship's name, Captain Tim! Go *Perseverance!*"

With that, Tim stood a little taller, turned to look out over the bow of
the *Perseverance*, and steered toward the mouth of Hardwork Harbor.
Just as he was about to turn on a course that would send him out to sea,
he spotted a smaller boat slowly making its way across the harbor. As
Tim approached, he realized the reason for the boat's slow speed; it was
following a channel dredger boat. The dredger would scoop up muck
and deposit it into the main cargo hold of the smaller boat. The smaller
vessel looked familiar to Tim. As he crept closer, he could make out the
captain on the bridge, who was sitting back in a chair with his feet on
the helm. He was driving his boat with his feet while talking on the radio. Tim was about to turn away when the foot-driving captain turned
and made eye contact.

For a moment his face didn't register with Tim, but the other captain
recognized Tim immediately. Stunned, he dropped the radio transmit-
ter as he hopped to his feet and went to his starboard bridge wing. His
mouth was wide open as he stood and stared with disbelief at the *Perseverance* gliding by. Tim nodded and gave Captain Ted a salute as if to
say, "You made your choice."

Ted's was the last face Tim saw when he left Hardwork Harbor.
He smiled as he thought about what he'd just witnessed. There was
Ted, Mr. Most Likely To Succeed, spending his days following a
channel dredger collecting muck. Tim wondered what excuses Ted
gave everyone for how he ended up being a muck collector.

Shortly after his ship left the harbor, with his bow headed on a
course toward the setting sun and the Big Island of the BYIs, Tim
looked up at the paddle and heard Captain Peter whisper in his ear,
"Your course in life is up to you!

HOW TO GET STARTED

Action #8: Team Up!

In the movie *Rambo,* Sylvester Stallone plays a soldier named John Rambo who conducts a series of missions all by himself. The lone soldier acts so independently that today's SEAL instructors often use the phrase "No Rambos" to define what a SEAL team is *not* about. Instructors used the phrase hourly during my training. They would remind us at every turn that SEALs don't work alone, but are part of a team that operates as one. No member is more important than another. Each one has a purpose, and when properly trained and focused, the team can achieve incredible results.

Before joining a SEAL team, you must prove to the instructors that you have the resolve to be there. One of the best tests for that resolve is Hellweek, which I went through in the sixth week of my 35-week training. Just hours before my Hellweek started, several instructors gave lectures about what it takes to be a SEAL. They presented two metaphors I will never forget. First, a Vietnam veteran SEAL compared SEAL training to the forging of a samurai sword: heat the metal, pound it with a hammer, stick it in cold water, and repeat the process approximately 2,000 times. He said no one can sustain that kind of punishment without first knowing *why* they want to be a SEAL. Knowing why enables the trainee to endure the pounding he receives. The second metaphor introduced us to Rambo. There are no Rambos, no lone soldiers, on a SEAL team. Rambos get people killed. SEALs succeed by remaining committed to their teams.

The importance of the team is stressed beginning on day one of SEAL training. Teams work together in every facet of training, from cleaning and eating to swimming and shooting. We even went to the bathroom as a team! The smallest SEAL team — the one that forms the foundation for the larger teams — consists of two swim buddies. Two swim buddy pairs make a fire team, two fire teams make a squad, and two squads make a platoon. (Today's SEAL nomenclature has changed slightly with the use of squadrons, but the concept remains the same — it's all about the team.) Just like a house, the teams within the larger SEAL team are built using two bricks at a time: swim pair by swim pair.

Your swim buddy does not stay with you upon graduation from SEAL training. Most graduates join different teams. Upon arriving with a new team, you start the process over by teaming up with a new swim buddy. This time, however, your swim buddy is part of a much bigger team. Eight swim pairs will join forces to create a platoon that will spend the next two years together preparing for and executing more than 150 different kinds of missions. (When my SEAL Team TWO platoon trained for our six-month deployment, we had to be prepared for 167 different missions.) Each SEAL team has different operating environments and different mission specialties, but the team dynamic remains the same: start with two-man teams and work your way up to a platoon team of sixteen men.

This same dynamic works whether you're starting a family or a company; it all starts with finding some kind of a "swim buddy." You want to find someone who is good at what you're not good at doing. While this may sound simple, the challenge comes when you look inside yourself to determine your weaknesses. It's not easy at first to admit you're not good at a particular skill, but over time you'll become comfortable with the concept. It took me awhile to come to grips with it. When you're young you believe you can do it all, but as you become aware of excellence around you, you begin to understand that you can't be excellent at everything. Some things come naturally. I've been comfortable from an early age with public speaking and storytelling, but finance is a different story. I struggled to learn the language and the concepts. Yet it's a critical component of running a successful business. While you should never stop trying to learn something that doesn't come easily for you, it's also important to acknowledge the things you find extra challenging. These are the things to keep in mind when looking for a teammate. You want to find teammates whose skills complement your own.

Teammates play another important role: They can help when you're feeling stuck. A teammate's attitude can make the difference between success and failure. When you're on your journey, not every day will be bright. You may even have more dark days than sunny days. There will be days when you question yourself, and days when nothing seems to go your way. A great teammate can be your perfect pick-me-up when you're feeling defeated. The challenge that has you stumped and feeling depressed may not have your teammate feeling the same way. It might even invigorate your teammate if the challenge requires skills that come naturally to that person. Before you know it you'll be over the next obstacle thanks to your teammate. Even if neither of you knows exactly what to do, your teammate might know an expert who can help conquer the obstacle in your path. Every one of my major accomplishments has depended on finding great teammates.

First, however, you must find your "why." Great people want to join an effort with a purpose; they need a reason to team up. If you don't have a firm handle on your why, how can you expect other talented people to understand why they should team up with you? Your why is your calling card for finding the perfect teammates to help make a dream a reality. Understanding your why and the work you've accomplished toward your goal is similar to SEAL training. It's proof of your resolve to complete the goal. No one wants to join a team that is going to fail. Everyone wants to be a winner. The ability to articulate your reason for going after your dream will help inspire others to join you. Finding the perfect teammates starts with a perfect understanding of your why.

This is the beauty of the U-PERSIST framework. Once you have a teammate, you can use the actions of U-PERSIST all over again. U-PERSIST works for teams as well as for individuals, and I believe your teammates will appreciate the framework. A funny thing happens when you create a team: your goals grow. They become team goals, and teams have a tendency to dream even bigger. When they do, you'll need U-PERSIST even more!

No matter what your goal, always remember that nothing great was ever achieved without a team. Period. No single person can do it all. Teaming up is an essential step in accomplishing your dream. It can be the difference between languishing with inaction and finding unbelievable success. It all starts with the first action of U-PERSIST: Understand your why. When you know *why* you're willing to work hard and take risks to achieve your goal, you'll be able to show others why they should team up with you. Once you have a teammate, you can attract more teammates, and then there is no limit to what you can accomplish. It all starts with a dream. So what are you waiting for? Dream as if everything is possible. Dream big and GO FOR IT!

About the Quotes

in *Be Unstoppable*

Captain Peter is a wise and well-read student, not only of the world, but also of the word. He draws some of his wisdom from many leaders who preceded him, as noted here:

Page 30: "I have learned to *'Trust but verify.'*" —President Ronald Reagan

Page 35: *"Whether you think you can, or think you can't – you're right."*
—Henry Ford

Page 49: *"The only real mistake is the one from which we learn nothing."*
—Henry Ford.

Page 51: *"Luck favors the prepared."* —Louis Pasteur

Page 53: *"Failure to plan is planning to fail."* —Benjamin Franklin

Page 76: *"Before you can achieve, you must believe!"* —William H. Johnsen

Page 84: *"Nothing in the world can take the place of persistence. Talent will not; nothing is more common than unsuccessful men with talent. Genius will not; un-rewarded genius is almost a proverb. Education will not; the world is full of educated derelicts. Persistence and determination alone are omnipotent. The slogan, 'Press On' has solved and always will solve the problems of the human race."*
—Calvin Coolidge.

Page 92: *"The mother of perfection is perfect repetition."*
—adapted from Ryan Straten

Page 111: *"Never ever give up."* —attributed to Winston Churchill

Page 133: *"Before the gates of excellence, the high gods have placed sweat."*
—Hesiod

145

Acknowledgments

I owe this book to the series of masters and commanders who taught me the Master and Commander Code over the past 45 years. They entered my life at just the right moments to help me with my navigation. They helped me plot a course out of the harbor, rebuild after running aground (sometimes after hitting rocks), and inspired me to modify my ship. They have been there through all the courses I've run in my life, steadfast supporters of my dreams. Without them, the Master and Commander Code wouldn't exist. They represent the best of me. They are:

Jennifer Ryan Mills, wife and teammate. Without her, I would have never left the harbor, got off the rocks, or rebuilt my ship. She's been by my side inspiring me from day one, providing course corrections at just the right moments, battening down the hatches for years on end, and always willing to continue the journey. She and my boys are the best things that have ever happened to me.

Paul and Swan Mills, my parents. They taught me to dream, to believe in myself and use creativity to solve problems. They opened my eyes to art in all its forms, and helped nudge me along the path to appreciate the power of an artistic mindset. Their encouragement, support, and love are what inspired me to choose my own course, to go after my dreams and to establish my own limits.

Joseph "Pops" Ryan, my father-in-law. He taught me how to make a dream come true. I learned the art of business, the definition of perseverance, and a passion for helping others succeed from him. He continues to teach me the blocking and tackling required to turn a dream into reality, and he is the definition of unconditional love and support.

William Hartwell Perry, Jr., my crew coach. He was much more than a coach; he was a mentor of boys aspiring to be men. He instilled in me, and hundreds like me, the makings of manhood and how to be a true teammate. He taught me how to pull hard on and off the water, how to win as a team, and no matter what, how to never stop pulling.

My SEAL team, my brotherhood. From my commanding officers to the chiefs and enlisted men who make everything happen I learned that limitations are made to be broken, that the power of the team will always prevail over the ego of the individual, and that freedom isn't free. I remain eternally thankful for the men and women who continue the work at the sharpest end of the spear.

Barton O'Brien, entrepreneur. He gave me the inspiration and direction to stay on my course when the winds seemed too strong, the waves too big. He provides radar when I can't see the course in front of me and sonar for those hidden obstacles just below the surface of my courses.

Steve G. Hauser, industrial designer. He taught me much more than form follows function, he showed me how to apply design thinking to more than just products; that the great joys of life come from designing a life worth living, and than even petty officer third class dental techs can achieve greatness!

Michael Cronan, artist. He is much more than a painter, musician, graphic artist, father, and husband. He inspired me to dream bigger while finding purpose within my dreams. He opened my eyes to the poetry of life and the magic of embracing the moment.

Tristram Coburn, my agent and publisher, for his consistent encouragement and course corrections. To a crew of remarkable shipmates — John Ross Bush, Jonathan Eaton, Dan Kirchoff, Thomas "Tommy" Rainwater, Stephanie Rach, and Janet Webb — were the experts and captains I needed to make this dream come true. Thank you Tris, John, Jon, Dan, Tommy, Stephanie, and Janet — I'd go to sea with you again any day! Also, a big thank you to my Teammates at Implus whose operational excellence and support have helped take this book to the next level.

And finally, and most profoundly, my boys—Henry, Charlie, John, and William. I wrote this book over four years of late nights and long flights. I used the code to accomplish this Milestone Goal. My "why" was clear — it was for you. I know of no greater "why" than the purpose of helping the next generation stand on our shoulders to make future generations better. Mom and I don't expect you to follow our course; we want you to follow your own courses. Your courses, your dreams, are entirely Up To You. You decide your journeys and your destinations. Just know we'll be there every step of the way, cheering you to Go For It! Dream big, work hard, have fun and Never, Ever Give Up on your dreams. We love you.

San Francisco–based Alden Mills began taking control of his life at age twelve, when his doctor told him to learn chess because his asthma would keep him from playing sports. His first goal was to conquer the asthma, and he went on to achieve extraordinary things in sports, academics, military service, business, and philanthropy. Alden became a nationally ranked rower, a gold medalist in the Olympic Festival, and captain of the freshman and varsity teams at the U.S. Naval Academy. As a Navy SEAL he led his platoon through multiple missions.

After discharge from the military, he founded Perfect Fitness and led it to growth of over 12,000%, annual sales of $90 million, and *Inc.* magazine recognition as the fastest-growing consumer products company in America in just three years. He developed over 40 patents, including the Perfect Pushup, Perfect Pullup, Perfect Situp, and Perfect Ab Carver.

Alden's books include *Be Unstoppable* and *Build Unstoppable Teams*. He has been featured on ABC's *Nightline, CBS This Morning, The Big Idea with Donny Deutsch,* and more. He serves on the boards of a number of non-profits.

For tools and resources to help you become unstoppable, visit Alden-Mills.com.